WE
ARE THE
PHARISEES

WE ARE THE PHARISEES

Kathleen Kern

HERALD PRESS
Scottdale, Pennsylvania
Waterloo, Ontario

Library of Congress Cataloging-in-Publication Data
Kern, Kathleen, 1962-
We are the Pharisees / Kathleen Kern.
p. cm.
Includes bibliographical references.
ISBN 0-8361-3671-3 (alk. paper)
1. Christian life—Mennonite authors. 2. Pharisees.
3. Christianity and anti-Semitism. 4. Pride and vanity. I. Title.
BV4501.2. K438 1995 94-28471
248.4'897—dc20 CIP

The paper used in this publication is recycled and meets the minimum requirements of American National Standard for Information Sciences—Permanence of Paper for Printed Library Materials, ANSI Z39.48-1984.

Library of Congress Catalog Number: 94-28471
International Standard Book Number: 0-8361-3671-3
Printed in the United States of America
Book design by James Butti

04 03 02 01 00 99 98 97 96 95 10 9 8 7 6 5 4 3 2 1

To my mother, Marilyn Rayle Kern,
who was right about the Pharisees
all along

Contents

Foreword

One of the most deeply entrenched assumptions I find among Christians is that the Pharisees of Jesus' day were legalistic hypocrites. However much Christians differ in other ways, one common—and tragic—piece of our heritage is a radically negative view of the early Jews who called themselves Pharisees.

Over the last several decades, our understanding of Judaism in the first century has changed dramatically. Manuscript discoveries at Qumran expanded the picture to include a group about which little had previously been known. Careful rereadings of the New Testament revealed the polemical nature of many comments about Jews. Fresh studies of Jewish writings confirmed the growing sense of the tremendous liveliness and diversity in early Judaism.

Despite these changes, the Pharisees continue to be perceived as wizened, narrow-minded, self-righteous creatures. Kathleen Kern addresses this problem with an engaging presentation of the historical evidence, carefully and sensitively laying out the problems with the way Christians think about Pharisees. She makes available a great deal of recent work in a way that will make it genuinely accessible.

But this is not simply a book of interest to antiquarians. As the title indicates, *We Are the Pharisees* concerns *us*. By means of anecdote and confession, Kern gently reminds us that the Pharisees were good, faithful, religious people of their day. And it is good, faithful, religious people of every era who find themselves in conflict with Jesus. Here the questions become deeply personal encounters with the claims of the gospel about who is truly good.

Kern helps the church face its responsibility to Jews and their traditions. Her study has important implications for how we preach and teach about Jews and Judaism. She does not shy away from revealing that we Christians have all too often purchased an exalted picture of Christianity by lying about our Jewish neighbors. Taking Kern's book seriously will mean a reexamination of the church's educational materials and sermon preparation and public statements.

This book begins with the apparently simple question, "Who were the Pharisees?" In the end, however, that question has metamorphosed into one that is far more profound, "What does it mean to love the neighbor?"

—Beverly Roberts Gaventa
Princeton Theological Seminary

Preface

I started this book originally to get down in writing what one of my friends at church calls my "Pharisee rant." I did not expect it to take over and lead me on the journeys it did. In the beginning, all I wanted to do was tell people that the Pharisees had gotten a bad rap historically, and that we should look for ourselves in Jesus' criticisms of the Pharisees.

As it was, reference led to reference, and I found myself greatly enriched by new contacts with the worlds of rabbinical studies, Dead Sea Scroll scholarship, and Jewish-Christian dialogue. They have given me new insights into the Bible and into the ways human beings have of relating with God and with each other.

I have written this book both to serve the individual reader and the group wishing to do a book study. It is my hope that the questions raised will also give the reader new insights into the Bible and into human relationships. I ask readers to join me in praying that a deeper understanding of the Scriptures will facilitate better relationships between Christians and Jews and that all of humanity will one day experience, to quote theologian Rosemary Radford Ruether, "a *shalom* without victims."

Acknowledgments

The bulk of my gratitude I owe to Susan and Victor Klassen, who not only read the manuscript and made suggestions, but also provided me with the home and family support which made it possible for me to write it. The Klassens and the rest of the Rochester Area Mennonite Fellowship, through their continuing interest and encouragement, helped me to bring this project to completion.

I would also like to thank the helpful library staff of the Webster Public Library and the Ambrose Swasey Library at Colgate Rochester Divinity School who aided me in my research. I acknowledge Dr. David Ruderman of Yale and Dr. Lawrence Schiffman of New York University, whose lectures in Rochester sent my research off in new directions. Dr. Jacob Rabinowitz read through the manuscript and checked for errors in "Jewish minutiae" (his words).

Special thanks also to my mother for reading and correcting the proofs of this manuscript while I was in Haiti during the summer and fall of 1994. She made it possible for the book to appear on schedule.

Finally, I would like to thank the biblical faculty of Colgate Rochester Divinity School, who instilled in me an appreciation for Judaism and a nagging desire for the truth. I especially want to acknowledge Dr. Beverly Roberts Gaventa (now of Princeton Theological Seminary) in whose New Testament Foundations class the origins for this book began percolating.

—*Kathleen Kern*
Webster, New York

1

We Are the Pharisees

Once upon a time, there lived a man who grew up on a farm in Nappanee, Indiana. He excelled both in sports and in academics and had many friends at school. He attended one of his denomination's colleges, where he met his future wife, a nursing major. Briefly he considered majoring in religious studies, with the idea of one day entering the pastoral ministry, but discovered after taking a business course that he had a knack in this area. After much prayer and reflection, he decided he could best serve God as a businessman.

The man's abilities in the business world soon made him and his family affluent. Although his wealth enabled him to make large donations to various charities, he felt dissatisfied in his vocation. Eventually, he took a position with his denomination's mutual aid association. He thanked God for the chance to use his abilities to help people in need.

The man and his wife loved and valued each other. They had three daughters, all of whom accepted Christ into their lives, partially because of their parents' influence. One daughter chose to become a missionary to Taiwan. Another chose to become a homemaker, and one chose to work with battered women in Chicago.

On a visit to his daughter in Chicago, he took a stroll through the neighborhood around the counseling center where she worked. On one corner stood an old stone church. Several once-gorgeous stained-glass windows had cardboard taped behind jagged holes. Pigeon droppings frosted the sills. Out in front stood a sign made of white plywood: CORNERSTONE COMMUNITY CHURCH, it read in neatly painted black letters.

The man tried the front door and found it unlocked. *Not a good idea in this neighborhood,* he thought. He walked inside the darkened sanctuary and saw a tile mosaic depicting Christ's crucifixion hanging behind the altar. A sense of ancient holiness filled the man, and he sat in the fourth pew from the front to pray.

He heard someone enter from the rear of the church, but did not open his eyes or raise his head until he heard loud sniffling noises.

A man knelt in front of the altar rail. After struggling to focus in the dim light, he recognized a local pimp his daughter had pointed out to him the night before. She had counseled several prostitutes who worked for this man. The pimp had treated these women with great violence, using their addiction to drugs to keep them dependent on him.

The businessman in the fourth pew thought about the human misery in which this man had trafficked. He pondered the endless cycle of poverty, brutality, and drug addiction that this man had perpetuated.

He then thought about his own life, the family he cherished, and his church to which he tithed fully from both his income and his personal time. He thought of his position as chair of the board of deacons that had made it possible for him to help the needy in his community.

He congratulated himself for providing a stable home

for his daughters and for bringing them up to desire lives of service to Christ. He knew that in at least a small way, he had made it possible for his youngest daughter to take this job in Chicago and help heal the victims of this pimp's violence.

"Thank you, Lord," he prayed, "for having made me who I am, for leading me along a righteous road, for giving me the gifts to serve you and the church. I am grateful that you have helped me set a good example for my children. I thank you for my daughter, who has dedicated herself to fighting the wickedness and misery that this pimp is responsible for. I thank you that I am not like this pimp here."

But the pimp, kneeling on the floor by the altar, began beating himself on the chest and sobbing, "God, be merciful to me, a sinner."

• • •

I learned a lot about Pharisees in Sunday school. Even as a small child, I knew they were the chief enemies of Jesus. They were sneaky, always looking for ways to trip Jesus up. Jesus, my hero, always foiled them in their attempts. I learned they did not care about poor people or sick people, that they loved a mysterious thing known as "the law" more than they loved God. I learned that they had no sense of humor.

You might imagine my confusion, then, when I listened in on a conversation my mother had with my grandparents and heard her refer to Pharisees as Jews. "The Pharisees weren't Jewish," I protested. "They were against the Jews." (I knew that Jesus was Jewish, so it seemed to make sense to assume that the Pharisees hated Jews.)

My mother explained to me that the Pharisees were not only Jewish but were, in fact, the "good Jews" of their time, the ones who really cared about pleasing God.

I had become accustomed to my parents putting a 180-degree spin on most of the facts I learned at church. So I mentally filed away my mother's seemingly eccentric statement for further consideration.

In my subsequent reading of the Scriptures, I looked for the goodness in the Pharisees and only found account after account of Jesus' wrath toward them. I decided that it was just one more thing in the Bible that I did not understand.

Years later, as a sophomore in college, I attended a seminar in Bogota, Colombia, on Latin American economics and liberation theology. I had never traveled outside the United States before and would have found the trip exciting in any event.

The reality far exceeded my expectation. For the first time in my life, I witnessed the squalor of absolute poverty. I saw children of five and six living in the streets. I met political prisoners. I met wealthy Colombians who thought any mention made of the rampant poverty around them was vulgar.

I learned about Christian base communities, where people, after working 12-16 hours a day, gathered in the evening for Bible study. I heard about how Christian love became an active force for change in these communities. I met people from these communities for whom choosing the way of Christ meant facing persecution, imprisonment, and possibly death.

After visiting one such community in Girardot, Colombia, the professor who had come down with us said, "It's like the Reformation happening all over." Indeed, I, too, felt a sense of joy and awe as I worshiped with people who had reclaimed the Bible from the powers that oppressed them, who had discovered that Christ's gospel was one of liberation, not of bondage.

When I came back to the United States, I wanted to tell

everyone of the insights and revelations that the trip to Colombia had given me. I felt that I had a message to deliver to the Christians of North America.

My Christian friends back at college listened with polite interest, but they had papers due and exams to study for. Some made halfhearted invitations: "That sounds really interesting. We'll have to get together. I'd like to hear more about it when I have more time." Invariably, that expression of interest marked the end of the discussion.

Likewise, several members of my church expressed their happiness at my having had this opportunity, but they had things to attend to—including the work of the church.

They were not just making excuses. There were Sunday school teachers to be found, quilts to be quilted, social justice groups to be organized, needy people in the community to be helped, volunteers for the local self-help shop to be enlisted.

And of course, there was that congregational meeting coming up. Members of the church were to vote on whether to carpet the sanctuary or build a new addition (or something else involving renovation of the church building). Those for and against felt strongly about their positions. Emotions were running high.

But you don't understand! I wanted to shout. *The kingdom of God is at hand! I have seen it myself. I have seen the Spirit of God working mighty things. I have witnessed Christian love in action! All the little things that keep you busy, what are they compared to the work of the Lord being done by our persecuted brothers and sisters in Latin America?*

Now, I want you to understand that my friends at college and the members of my church had a deep commitment to Christ. My church was a vibrant and active church that ministered to the needs of hundreds of people—both members and nonmembers.

I joined this church when I was nineteen and felt a strong sense of having come home at last. The people of that congregation made me feel loved and nurtured and valued. They gave of themselves in many different ways and inspired me to desire a life of service to Christ.

All the more reason, I thought, for them to receive my personal revelations with enthusiasm. One does not merely show polite interest when a fellow member has told of a recent encounter with the kingdom of God.

And then I understood the Pharisees.

I understood how the Pharisees could be both the good "churchgoing" people of their time and the Jews who brought Jesus' wrath upon themselves.

The average Pharisee was no more hardhearted, unloving, or hypocritical than the average churchgoing North American. Members of both groups felt strongly about their beliefs. Both were intensely concerned about pleasing God. Both could become so caught up in the details of their religious life that they could forget or ignore the real presence of God in their midst.

• • •

This book has come about slowly. In the eleven years since I had that first revelation about the nature of Pharisees, I have gone to seminary. There I learned more about the first-century Jewish milieu that gave birth to the New Testament. I have moved to a city with several Jewish temples and developed relationships both personally and professionally with Jews.

I have also heard too many sermons preached with casual references to the pride or legalism of the Pharisees—so different, of course, from our own pride and legalism. When I hear the word "Pharisee" mentioned by anyone, I wince with the expectation of negative comments to follow, for the secular and religious world alike perpetuate this negative myth. My dictionary, for example, defines the adjective "pharisaical" as "marked by hypocritical censorious self-righteousness."[1]

I believe we need to gain a better understanding of the Pharisees for the following reasons:

1. In studying the Jewish culture of the centuries immediately preceding and following the birth of Christ, we gain a better understanding of how the New Testament came into being. When we understand the New Testament better, we are more able to receive God's revelation to us through Scripture.

2. As a result of the bad press Pharisees have historically received, we often assume they were all alike. When we use the Pharisees as examples of rigidity, legalism, and self-righteousness, we are guilty of stereotyping. If we have decided that not all Orientals are inscrutable and not all white Anglo-Saxon Protestants are bigoted and uptight, then we should also cease using adjectives like "proud," "hypocritical," or "legalistic" to refer to all Pharisees.

3. When we think of the harsh sayings of Jesus as relevant only to a Jewish sect of the first century, we forget to look at ourselves in the light of these teachings. We neglect to examine our own haughtiness, pride, and rigidity when we attribute these qualities to the Pharisees.

4. Throughout the centuries, people have used the references to the Pharisees in the New Testament as justification for persecuting Jews. Hitler had Christian theologians and biblical scholars writing anti-Semitic propaganda for him. This fact alone should impel us to look at Jesus' words on the Pharisees in a more radical way. These verses have been used to hurt and destroy others. We need to learn to use them to empower and help others.

5. Members of historic Anabaptist churches can find interesting parallels between their history and Jewish history. Both regard God's revelation as it appears in the Scriptures as the primary focus of their faith. Both have faced persecution for their faith.[2] Both have chosen to separate themselves from mainstream society in different ways. When we find parallels between our own experiences and those of another people, we can learn to be more loving, humble, and humane in our dealings with that group.

I would ask the reader to keep the title of this book in mind while reading the following chapters. Even as we explore cultural influences from another time and place, let us bear in mind that we share with the Pharisees a love of God and a desire to serve this God—who chose a Jewish carpenter to preach the good news of God's redemption.

For Discussion

1. To whom do you feel superior? Try to answer honestly. Even if you do not *want* to feel superior to these people, try to choose an example, such as one of these:

gambler s
developmentally disabled people
liberals
Republicans
Progressive Conservatives
New Democrats
rich people
life insurance salespeople
doctors who perform abortions
child molesters
rapists
garbage collectors
golfers
drug dealers
capitalists
welfare recipients
fundamentalists
conservatives
Democrats
Liberals (party)
politicians in general
poor people
telephone marketers
feminists
non-Christians
intellectuals
psychotics
soldiers
functional illiterates
socialists

Now, try to recast the parable of Luke 18:9-14 to fit your life situation. Ask yourself about certain things you do or say that you believe are pleasing to God. Do you help out with a youth group? Volunteer to help the needy? Donate gifts of time and money to your church? Work hard on your parenting skills?

Imagine yourself in the same position as the Christian businessman at the beginning of the chapter. What are some situations where you might meet one of the people you consider despicable? Why do you feel superior to this person?

2. Have there been times in your life when someone surprised you by being more spiritual than you thought?

3. What did you learn about Pharisees while growing up? What were your sources? Sunday school? Family? Books? Has what you learned affected your attitude toward Jews in general? Why or why not?

4. How would you judge the state of Jewish-Christian relations in the world today? What are questions you might want to ask a Jewish person if you had the opportunity? Do you feel any responsibility for Christian persecution of the Jews throughout history? Why or why not?

2

First-Century Palestine

The following is an excerpt from H. Darrell Ndusha's *Archaeological Perspectives on Sub-Canada from the Pre-Cataclysmic Era*—a textbook that will be published six thousand years from tomorrow:

Religion

Our understanding of the religious practices of the people who lived in the coastal city of Columbus and its surrounding region is necessarily limited by two major factors.

1. Just as the Great Cataclysm forever buried many secular artifacts that might yield a coherent understanding of the people who lived in the eastern part of Sub-Canada, so it is with religious artifacts as well. Some have conjectured that the true cultural and religious centers of the region were located in eastern cities lost to the ocean. Numerous expeditions to the Atlantic Ocean floor have failed to uncover evidence of these cities. Hence, we will operate on the generally accepted belief that Columbus was a religious center, of sorts, for the loose confederation of nation states occupying the territory of sub-Canada.

2. Columbus was situated in the province known as Ohio, one of the nation states occupying the region between the greater powers of Canada and Mexico. Because

of the relative unimportance of these nation states except as trading routes between the two larger nations, little has survived to tell us about the customs, dress, daily life, or religion of the inhabitants of the region around Columbus.

These exceptions being noted, there is enough archaeological data available to enable us to postulate three major religious movements in Columbus and its surrounding region.

We believe that the largest sect of the late Christian era in Sub-Canada was that of **Catholicism**. Expeditions in the area of Columbus have uncovered several fine examples of Catholic temples. Archaeologists have uncovered at these sites the gold crosses, colored glass windows, and ritualistic vessels typical of Catholic temples from this period. The sites of these temples vary in size and in the amount of ornamentation found. Some speculate that these differences indicate a strict social class structure in Columbian society and within the Catholic Church itself. This speculation, however, does not satisfactorily explain the proliferation of different types of temples.

For example, archaeologists have uncovered three Catholic temples that have the word "Methodist" engraved in their cornerstones. In two of the sites, the surviving infrastructures indicate rather small buildings existed there. Yet another Catholic "Methodist" temple within a five-square-kilometer community would have been a huge structure for its time, capable of accommodating more than a thousand worshipers or pilgrims. Many scholars now believe that the titles of "Methodist," "Baptist," and so on, refer mostly to different ritualistic emphases.

Another popular religion, dubbed "**Americanism**" because of an apparent nationalism integrated into its rituals, was widely practiced throughout sub-Canada. The deity worshiped was symbolized by a banner hung on a pole, often with a bronzed or gold eagle capping the pole. Interesting examples of syncretism have been found in the Columbus area. Many of the Catholic temples contained banner poles with eagles in the same locus where diggers found gold crosses. In one temple a few shreds of red and white fabric derived from petroleum were also found preserved.

Of considerable interest to both archaeologists and the general public was the discovery in 4405 P.C.[1] of a small temple hermetically preserved in a lava flow.

There is very little written about the **Jehovah's Witnesses** in the limited number of documents surviving from this era. However, judging from the number of pamphlets and writings contained within this site, we can conclude that Jehovism must have had a wide influence throughout the region. Almost nothing is known, however, about the rituals of Jehovism.

• • •

When archaeologists uncover a clay tablet and discover that it contains an inventory for sacks of grain received by a certain merchant, they feel like celebrating. When they turn up a fragment of a preserved papyrus that contains a recipe or a letter, they become giddy with delight.

Why? Such a find is called a **primary source.** Historians value primary sources because they provide objective bits of information from the era the historians wish to study. An invoice for sacks of grain might provide insight into the dietary habits and economy of a certain region. A fragment of a letter written by a soldier in Palestine to his wife in Rome might provide a clue to the ordinary domestic routine of people who did not occupy the "important" levels of society.

If you were to go into any average seminary library to look for a history of Palestine in the century preceding and the century following the birth of Jesus Christ, you would find a fair amount of material available to you. You might even think that the number of books on the library shelf shows that many primary sources from or about Palestine during this era are available to historians.

In truth, historians have access to a relatively skimpy amount of material relating to Judaism or Christianity from the first century A.D. Much has survived from the great empires of Egypt, Greece, and Rome. However, except for a few references to Palestine in their histories, little objective information about the inhabitants of this region exists.

The importance of Palestine to Rome essentially lay in its being on the way to Egypt. Those of us who love the Bible, who think of its birthplace as the Holy Land, find it hard to imagine the historical obscurity of this region. The habits of those backward people who called themselves Jews held scant interest for the average Roman. Therefore we have few reports about the customs, dress, or religious practices of the inhabitants of Palestine. The reader should regard the information that follows as hypothetical and based on the conjectures of scholars.[2]

• • •

Historians have traditionally divided first-century Judaism into four factions:[3]

We know little about the faith of the *'am ha'arets*[4]—the ordinary Jewish farmers or laborers. We have reason to believe that they traveled to Jerusalem to offer sacrifices in the temple, but they did not leave much behind for historians to study. Because most written histories are skewed to represent the lives of the rich and powerful, we often have a distorted view of what life was like for ordinary people in any given period.

We also know very little about the *Sadducees.* Some believe they were a party for the upper classes: rich merchants, landowners, and priests. As political leaders, they enjoyed cordial relations with the Roman empire. They took a conservative approach to Scripture, acknowledging only the Torah (the first five books of the Bible) as divinely inspired. Some historians have speculated that their conservatism regarding Scripture sprang from their desire to maintain the status quo both politically and religiously. As long as people needed to offer sacrifices in the temple, those controlling the temple would wield considerable influence.

The *Essenes* showed their disgust with an immoral society by withdrawing from it and founding ritualistically pure communities. The Essenes believed that they were living in the end times and that the Messiah would be coming soon to deliver them from the Romans. Many historians think that the Jewish community which produced the Dead Sea Scrolls (found near Qumran, south of Jericho) was Essene.

Recent research has found clues that the Essenes at Qumran were originally Sadducees who left Jerusalem in 152 B.C., believing that many of their group had accommodated too much to Greek culture. From the context of the scrolls, it seems as though they were also unhappy about the Pharisees raising oral tradition up to the same level as Scripture (see below). Moving out to the community on the banks of the Dead Sea enabled them to practice a more purely "Jewish" religion.[5]

The root meaning of the term *Pharisee* is unclear. Many believe that it derives from a Hebrew or Aramaic term meaning "the separated ones." The Pharisees did seek to separate themselves from mainstream society so that they could live more faithfully. As lay scholars, they studied the Scriptures rigorously and developed an oral tradition to make the meaning of the Scriptures more accessible.

Pharisees became known for their pious living and for their scholarly abilities. They also believed in the resurrection of the dead (a concept which the Sadducees vigorously rejected). The Pharisees upheld the radical notion that ordinary Jews did not need to rely on priests for the primary expression of their religion. They could please God by living holy lives.

Destruction of the Temple

During A.D. 66-70 the Jews of Jerusalem revolted against Roman rule. In 70, the Romans destroyed the temple in Jerusalem—a catastrophe of immeasurable proportions for all Jews and for the emerging Christian church.

The temple served as a religious, cultural, and political center for the Jews of Palestine. Every Jew, from tenant farmer to the wealthiest landowner, viewed the temple as the place where heaven and earth intersected. Through daily prayers and sacrifices offered there, the people of Israel kept the laws of the Torah and thereby served their God.

With the temple gone, the ordinary people of Palestine lost the central expression of their faith. The Sadducees lost the source of their power and the reason for their existence. Historians have speculated that the Romans slaughtered the Essene communities in A.D. 70 because of their active resistance.[6]

That left the Pharisees. Since their attention had begun to shift from the temple to a focus upon the Scriptures and oral tradition regarding the Scriptures, the destruction of the temple did not devastate their faith. They saw the destruction as a tragedy, but found that its loss did not prevent them from serving God by living holy lifestyles according to the Scripture. In doing so, they fulfilled God's expectations, as expressed in the ancient prophetic message: "For I desire steadfast love and not sacrifice, the knowledge of God rather than burnt offerings."[7]

Sources on the Pharisees

As mentioned earlier in the chapter, we do not have many sources of information available to us about the religious customs of the people in Palestine. We have no primary sources at all about the Pharisees—unless one counts the reference Paul makes to himself as a Pharisee in Philippians 3:5 (written around A.D. 61-63).

We have basically three historical sources available to us about the Pharisees: Josephus, the Talmud, and the Gospels. With the exception of the Gospel of Mark (generally dated at 65-70), all three sources probably achieved final written form after A.D. 70.[8]

The Jewish historian *Josephus,* in two major works, *The War of the Jews* (75-79, with parts written later) and *The Antiquities of the Jews* (about 93) gives a largely favorable account of the Pharisees and their history. Historians do not regard him as wholly reliable because of his adeptness at political maneuvering. Born around A.D. 37-38, he led the Jewish revolt in Galilee in 66.

He was captured by the Romans and appears to have saved himself by telling Vespasian, the commander who captured him, that he would be emperor some day. The position of Roman emperor had a high turnover rate in the first century. Two years later, Vespasian did indeed become emperor. At that time, he released Josephus, who became a translator and historian for the Romans.

Josephus wrote *The War of the Jews* as propaganda. In it, he sought to convince his Jewish readers that they should not blame Rome for the destruction of the temple. He defended the Romans' political administration of Palestine and supported their reasons for crushing the Jewish uprising. Josephus said the Jews had brought the destruction of the temple upon themselves.

As one might suspect, he was living in Rome when he wrote this as well as his other works. His writings show a bias for the status quo and the governing classes. When describing Pharisees in history, he becomes critical of them at the times when they disrupted established order.[9]

In both *War* and *Antiquities,* Josephus sought to give his Roman readers some understanding of Jewish history. He associated the three predominant Jewish sects of his time with the philosophical schools so important in Greco-Roman thought. He also described the Pharisees as the predominant religious and political faction in Palestine and the one most worthy of the Romans' support.

The largest body of information regarding the Pharisees appears in the *Talmud,* a collection of oral teachings on the Torah handed down by the rabbis for several generations. The Talmud is divided into the *Mishnah,* the first written summary of the Oral Law, and the *Gemara,* the commentary on the Mishnah written by rabbinical scholars (*Talmud* became a synonym for *Gemara*).

There were two separate schools of these scholars, and so we have both Palestinian and Babylonian Talmuds. The Mishnah was completed around A.D. 200. The Palestinian Talmud was completed around 400-450, and the Babylonian Talmud around 500-600.[10] In a way, the Talmud compares to the New Testament, in that both built upon the theology of the Hebrew Bible and both enabled believers to remain true to their faith in the ensuing centuries.

The most limited source—and the one of most concern to this book—is that of the *New Testament.* In it, we find described the relationships that both Jesus and Paul had with the Pharisees, and we learn about certain laws that the Pharisees thought important to keep. As mentioned earlier, the dating of the Gospels is a matter of conjecture. Some time between A.D. 64 and 100 would encompass most hypotheses.

Origin and Destiny of the Pharisees

Using the three sources available to us, we can draw a brief sketch of the Pharisees' origin and what became of them after the temple fell.

In 166 B.C., a family of Jews known as the Maccabees began a military resistance against the despotic reign of Antiochus IV Epiphanes, a Greek ruler of a territory that included Syria and Palestine. Antiochus, slow to tolerate and quick to torture, had made punishable by death the rite of circumcision and the observance of the Sabbath.

This king had an altar to Zeus erected in the temple at Jerusalem, and he encouraged Gentiles to have sexual intercourse with prostitutes and other women inside the temple precincts. He ordered pigs and other unclean beasts sacrificed in the sanctuary and forced Jews to eat their flesh.[11] Small wonder, then, that the people of Palestine regarded the Maccabees as heroes and submitted to their authority when they liberated and cleansed the temple in 164 B.C.

The Maccabees fought on to gain political independence for Israel in 142 B.C. They and their successors, the Hasmonaeans, ruled Palestine as an independent Jewish state until 63 B.C., when the Romans took over. John Hyrcanus assumed the throne of his family in 135 B.C. and reigned till 104. Unlike his father and his uncles, John Hyrcanus emulated the Greek rulers of his time and sought to expand the borders of his territory. He conquered the coastal plain, Galilee, Samaria, and Idumea.[12] His son, Alexander Jannaeus, married Salome Alexandra, in whose hands Jannaeus left the government of Palestine upon his death.

In *Antiquities*, Josephus indicates that the Pharisees were a religious and political party during the period that the Hasmoneans ruled Palestine. Under queen Salome Alexandra (76-67 B.C.), they became the primary political force in the region.

After the death of the queen, her sons fought between themselves to rule Palestine. The Roman general Pompey supported first Aristobulus and then Hyrcanus II (63-40 B.C.). Hyrcanus also enlisted the support of Antipater, ruler of Idumea and father of Herod the Great (37-4 B.C.), who ruled Palestine when Jesus was born. The Romans entered Jerusalem in 63 B.C. and brought an end to its status as an independent Jewish state. From this time until the collapse of the Roman empire, puppet kings and Roman governors ruled the territory of Palestine.

Having lost their political power, the Pharisees continued as a school of thought within Judaism. Actually, they continued as several schools of thought. The two major teachers within Pharisaism at this time were Hillel and Shammai, who frequently disagreed with each other over ways to interpret the Torah. The Talmud records many of these disagreements. The school of Hillel outlasted the school of Shammai, so the records from the Talmud generally show Hillel coming out as the winner in the disputes between the two men. He seems to have transformed the Pharisees from a political party to a fellowship concerned with ritualistic purity in all aspects of life.[13]

After Jerusalem fell and the temple was destroyed in A.D. 70, the Pharisees founded an academy at Jabneh,[14] under the guiding hand of Yoanan ben Zakkai. At this academy, the rabbis began assembling stories which would later appear in the Talmud. They were also evaluating the many religious writings available and defining what constituted "Scripture."[15] The Pharisees agreed to accept Roman rule and discourage rebellion in exchange for the freedom to practice their religion.

The academy at Jabneh ceased to exist around A.D. 125. After the second Jewish revolt in the years 132-135, the Emperor Hadrian ordered all Jews to leave Jerusalem and not to return upon pain of death. Deprived not only of their temple but also their homeland, the Jews of Palestine emigrated to countries throughout the empire. Along with their possessions, they bore their love of God, their desire to remain faithful to God, and the knowledge of the Scriptures that would enable them to do so. Judaism survives to this day because of the Pharisees.

The Pharisees in the New Testament

The next chapter will explore more fully the status and function of the Pharisees in the New Testament. Before doing so, however, we will address the question of why the New Testament contains such harsh criticisms of the Pharisees and Jews in general.

We need to understand that the Gospels did not achieve final written form in a vacuum. During the time that the teachings and life history of Jesus were collected and written down—between A.D. 40 and 100—the early Christian church still had a strong connection to Judaism.

As the Christian movement began to spread throughout the Roman empire to Jews and Gentiles alike, conflicts began to arise between different Christian factions. We can see in the letters of Paul, written between A.D. 50 and 60, that some Christians wanted to retain close ties to Judaism. They required of their followers that they follow the Jewish dietary laws and continue certain rituals such as circumcision. Paul wrote some heated reprimands to Christians in Galatia for insisting that Gentile converts be circumcised before they could join the church.[16] From John 16:2 and Acts 14:1-7, we learn of the anger the Jews felt toward the Christians. As a result of that anger, they excluded Christians from their synagogues and even resorted to violence.[17]

As anyone with brothers and sisters can attest, the most intense kind of rivalry exists between siblings. We can forgive the failings of friends and acquaintances far more easily than we can forgive such failings in our brothers and sisters. Likewise, we can often overlook differences we have with friends and acquaintances more easily than we can the differences we have with members of our family.

My sister and I both accepted Jesus Christ as preteens, and when it comes to fundamentals of the Christian faith, we basically believe the same things. Yet we have had emotional arguments about religious issues. Sometimes the disputes centered on doctrines; sometimes they centered on how we put our Christian principles into practice. Occasionally the arguments degenerated into disagreeing over what was in good taste and what in poor taste.

Many friends and people I respect probably would have agreed with my sister's position on these matters. Yet my discussions with them never achieved the same emotional pitch that the discussions with my sister did. I did not feel the urgent need to change my friends as I did to "convert" my sister.

Why? Because I loved my sister, and because I loved Jesus Christ. The feelings I had for my sister were stronger than my feelings for others with whom I disagreed. My belief in Christ and how that affected my life mattered deeply to me.

In the first century after Jesus' death, Jews, Jewish Christians, and Gentile Christians had close connections with each other. They worshiped the same God. They earnestly desired to serve God and sought help from the Scriptures in doing so. They had to seek ways of preserving their faith within the context of Roman domination.

They disagreed with each other as to how these things should be accomplished. "Disagree" probably does not touch the depths of emotion involved. They yelled, they screamed, they squabbled, they fought, they excluded each other.

Consider some of the Talmudic references to Jewish

Christians, whom the rabbinical writers included under the classification of *minim*—heretics:

> May there be no hope for the apostates, and mayest thou speedily uproot the insolent government [Rome] in our days. And may the Nazarenes [Jewish Christians] and the Minim [Jewish heretics] die in a moment, may they be blotted out of the book of life and not be enrolled with the righteous. Praised be thou, Lord, who dost humble insolence.[18]
>
> Rabbi Simon ben Laqish said that a Gentile who observed the Sabbath is deserving of death. . . . Rabbi Yohanan said that a Gentile who engaged in the study of the Torah is deserving of death as it is said in Scripture, "Moses commanded us Torah as an inheritance" (Deuteronomy 33:4)—an inheritance for us, not for them.[19]
>
> We do not save from fire (on the Sabbath) the Gospels and the books of the *minim* ("heretics"). Rather, they are burned in their place.[20]

As you might imagine, feelings got very, very hurt.

When we read the New Testament, we need to remember that the Christians who collected the teachings of Jesus and wrote them down in final form still bore fresh wounds. Certain Jews had rejected them because of their belief that the Messiah had come in the person of Jesus Christ. When we read Paul's denunciations of the Jews, we need to remember that certain Jewish leaders had wanted him dead.[21] Certain Jewish Christians had put obstacles in his way as he sought to bring the good news of Jesus Christ to the known world.[22]

Because the followers of the one true God in the first century had closer relationships with each other than they did with pagans, their rivalry with each other was more intense. Because the things they believed mattered so much to them, they thought it important to convert or change their "misguided" brothers and sisters. The anger that developed because of these conflicts found its way into the New Testament.

Jesus and Paul

Jesus was Jewish. Paul was Jewish.

These statements may seem obvious. They appear here because certain Christians throughout the centuries have used the teachings of Jesus and Paul to justify persecution of the Jews.

We cannot possibly understand or appreciate the teachings of Jesus Christ unless we acknowledge that they came directly from the Hebrew Bible. His grief and anger at finding his words rejected stemmed from the fact that it was the people with whom he had the most in common who did the rejecting. Some who religiously studied the laws of Moses were the ones who turned away from his insights on these laws.

Nowhere in Paul's letters does he say, "I used to be a Jew." Indeed, in several of his letters he proclaims his Jewishness because some of his critics had called it into question.[23] Again, the "sibling rivalry" that occurred during the infancy of the Christian church had a big effect on Paul's thinking. His belief that the death of Christ had made certain Jewish rituals obsolete angered both Christian Jews and non-Christian Jews. He himself became angry when Christian Jews made certain Jewish rituals a requirement for becoming a Christian.

The emotional statements of Paul found in his letters, however, do nothing to contradict the fact that Paul was born Jewish and maintained his identity as a Jew until the day he died.

The use of the teachings of Jesus and Paul to justify persecution or hatred of the Jews (or anyone else, for that matter) is not just a matter of poor interpretation of the New Testament. It is blasphemy.

For Discussion

1. If aliens sealed your church building in a plastic bubble tomorrow, what conclusions might archaeologists draw from digging it up two thousand years later? What "primary sources" (such as church bulletins, newsletters, office memos) would prove of most interest to them? What are some mistaken assumptions they might make regarding the people who live in your region if they used your church as their main source of information?

2. In *From Politics to Piety: The Emergence of Pharisaic Judaism*, Jacob Neusner writes,

> We have many theories, but few facts, sophisticated theologies but uncritical, naive histories of Pharisaism which yield heated arguments unillumined by disciplined, reasoned understanding. Progress in the study of the growth of Pharisaic Judaism before 70 AD will depend upon . . . a determined effort to cease theorizing about the age. We must honestly attempt to understand not only what was going on in the first century, but also—and most crucially—how and whether we know anything at all about what was going on.[24]

This chapter briefly discussed four factions of Judaism in first-century Palestine. There may have been dozens of smaller factions. The practice of Judaism in the southern part of the country around Jerusalem probably differed greatly from the practice of Judaism up north, in Galilee. We simply do not know for sure because of the lack of information available to us.

How does *not* knowing much about first-century Palestine affect what we believe or do not believe about Jesus Christ?

Does it disturb you that many of the questions regarding this time period cannot be answered with certainty? Why or why not?

3. What are some behaviors and beliefs you tolerate better in casual acquaintances than you do in family members?

4. Why do schisms occur within churches? Have you ever experienced a church splitting apart because of a theological disagreement? Can you think of ways to prevent the bitterness such schisms produce?

3

Overlooked Pharisees

The denomination's workers in a certain country always looked forward to the annual missionaries' retreat in the capital city. This year, their denominational mission board had sent an exciting young speaker to present the program. He had caused a stir in theological circles back home by saying that the Gospels showed how God had a bias for the poor and powerless.

The missionaries were anxious to hear what this speaker had to say. If asked, they would have had to admit that they expected him to give them a pat on the back for the work they did among the poor in this country. The churches they planted had grown enormously in the last two decades. Hadn't they empowered natives to serve as leaders within the church? With their church camping program alone, they had brought over a thousand young people to Christ every summer for the last six years.

The speaker disappointed them. After addressing them briefly and finding out about their work in the country, he disappeared for the rest of the retreat. People saw him in the local tavern drinking beer and apparently enjoying himself in the company of people with whom the members of their church normally did not associate.

In the weeks that followed, he offended nearly all the leaders of this church, both natives and missionaries. He told them that they had become so obsessed with the details of administering the church that they had forgotten the original purpose of establishing the church there.

On one notable Sunday, this speaker took over the pulpit of the denomination's largest church and tore up the report that the country's missionary coordinators had sent to the denominational mission board. This report had proposed closing down clinics operated by the denomination and expanding the Christian camping program. Since the operation of the latter saved more souls, one of the country's coordinators had suggested that this program was more cost-effective. In denouncing this report as blasphemous, the young man made permanent enemies of several leading missionaries.

His popularity grew, however, among many members of the church in that country. Soon, many of the smaller churches began to wonder whether they should withdraw as members of this denomination and start an independent national church.

Several of the missionaries had themselves felt some concern over the direction their mission program was heading in this country. As individuals, they invited the young man to dinner, curious to hear what he had to say. The things he said often made them feel uncomfortable. He challenged them to scrutinize their motives for becoming missionaries. Still, these people tried to encourage the other missionaries to listen to what the young man had to say. They saw how the lay people in the congregations responded to his message, and they did not want to see a schism in their church.

Despite their efforts, nearly half the churches withdrew

and formed a new church, *Las Communidades de los Cueros Nuevos*—the New [Wine]skins Communities. So appalled were the missionary coordinators by this development that they conspired with the military junta that governed the country to kill the young man. These missionaries argued convincingly that he was a subversive and represented a threat to the established order.

After his death, the members of the New Wineskins Communities became more cautious, but their numbers grew all the more rapidly. The denominational mission board became concerned about the influence they had on the people who still considered themselves members of its church. Anyone who appeared to advocate the goals of the New Wineskins Communities was condemned as a heretic and excommunicated. Many missionaries felt some sympathy for New Wineskins, but learned not to discuss it.

The missionary board eventually appointed Paulina Yoder to begin investigating the churches that promoted the New Wineskins heresy. Paulina's parents had come to the country as newlyweds, and she had lived all her life there, except for the four years she studied at her denomination's college in the States. She was bright, spoke Spanish like a native (which in fact she was), and had used her education to further the work of the church in many ways.

Churches within the denomination began to fear her visits, because Paulina stood ready to jump on any slip of the tongue indicating sympathy with New Wineskins. Some unfortunates became grist for her inquisitions and found themselves excommunicated from the church they loved because they were not theologically "pure" enough. Many of them joined the New Wineskins Communities.

The remarkable transformation of Paulina Yoder occurred suddenly on a bus trip she made to the denominational headquarters in the country. In later years, opinion was divided over what happened, but after that trip, Paulina became a member of New Wineskins. She traveled over the entire Central and South American continent, preaching the gospel and starting numerous New Wineskins communities.

Toward the end of her life, she wrote the following to one of the communities in Uruguay:

"If anyone could speak for the [insert denominational name], I could.

"My parents were missionaries in the country before I was born, and I grew up learning all the correct theology and missiology. I was schooled at ___________ College and excelled in all my studies.

"Yet whatever gains I had, these I have come to regard as loss because of Christ."

• • •

Sometime after his ordination to the priesthood in 1524, Menno Simons read the Bible—not a normal activity for most priests during the sixteenth century. In particular, he searched through it to find support for the Roman Catholic doctrine of transubstantiation, which said that the bread and wine offered in communion became the actual flesh and blood of Jesus Christ. He found nothing in the Bible that supported this doctrine.

Sometime later, when he heard that the authorities had beheaded a man in the nearby town of Leeuwarden for becoming rebaptized, he again turned to Scripture and found no support for the sacrament of infant baptism. Eventually, the revelations from Scripture caused him to break with the Catholic Church and join the Anabaptist movement.[1]

At this point some people might be tempted to say, "Well, that's just the way the Catholic Church is. In our tradition, we read the Bible carefully."

Yet it may come as a surprise to you that the Bible also says positive things about the Pharisees. Years of sermons and Sunday school teachings have taught many of us that the Pharisees were bad men. Many of us grew up believing these teachings without ever really reading what the Bible has to say about them. We remember clearly the references to the Pharisees as a "brood of vipers" (Matt. 3:7; 23:33) or "whitewashed tombs" (23:27), but we forget verses which do not condemn the Pharisees. The New Testament, in reality, has many "value-neutral" references to them and even some, as mentioned above, that show them in a positive light.

Positive Attitudes Toward the Pharisees

Admittedly, we find no passages in the New Testament that one could subtitle, "The Pharisees: What a swell bunch of guys!" However, consider the story in Luke 5:17-26 (cf. Mark 2:1-12; Matt. 9:1-8).

The first thing we read is that Pharisees and "teachers of the law" ("scribes" of the Pharisees, Luke 5:21) have come "from every village of Galilee and Judea and from Jerusalem" to hear Jesus teach. Their presence indicates a certain amount of respect as well as curiosity. The sophisticated Jewish leaders and teachers from Jerusalem would not have shown up to hear just any religious fanatic or self-proclaimed prophet. Indeed, the area encompassing Galilee, Jerusalem, and Judea was about the size of Vermont. Since most people then traveled by foot or donkey, it took commitment and effort to travel such distances to hear someone teach.

While Jesus is teaching, some people lower a paralyzed man through the roof for Jesus to heal. He tells the man that his sins are forgiven. To the reader, the Pharisees seem to cast themselves in a negative light by thinking, "Who is this who is speaking blasphemies? Who can forgive sins but God alone?" Note, however, that the Pharisees do not say, "Jesus, you are a blasphemer." They are asking themselves a question. They *really want to know* how it is that this dynamic teacher can forgive sins.

When Jesus perceives their thoughts and gives an answer, we see no record of them arguing with him. Jesus says, "So that you may know that the Son of Man has authority on earth to forgive sins, . . . I say to you [the one paralyzed], stand up and take your bed and go to your home." When the paralyzed man walks, we read, "Amazement seized *all of them*, and they glorified God and were filled with awe, saying, 'We have seen strange things today' " (italics added).

The Pharisees—those cold legalistic nitpickers—are filled with wonder at Jesus' miracle and glorify God because of it. They do not begin to plot against him or in any way denigrate the miracle. They behave just as we would expect any Bible-believing people might when confronted by a living testimony to the grace of God.

The Gospel of Luke speaks of three instances in which individual Pharisees invited Jesus over for meals.[2] No doubt some of them regretted it afterward! It is no small thing to be told that you are full of "greed and wickedness" by a guest who has not had the courtesy to wash his hands before he partakes of your food (Luke 11:37-41).[3] In the two other accounts of Jesus responding to a Pharisee's dinner invitation, he says things less harsh. He anticipates what his hosts are thinking and uses the visit as an opportunity to teach. Indeed, Simon the Pharisee addresses Jesus respectfully as "Teacher" (Luke 7:40), in spite of the fact that Jesus has welcomed a woman of ill repute into the company of his dinner companions.

Too often in the past, people have focused on the "comeuppance" Jesus gives to the Pharisees who have invited him to dinner. We do not take in the whole picture, however, unless we consider that the Pharisees *invited* Jesus to dinner in the first place. We give no credit to the Pharisees for their hospitality, nor do we consider that they probably invited him because they wanted to hear what he had to say.

In another often-overlooked passage, the Pharisees come to Jesus to warn Jesus that Herod wishes to kill him. As with the Pharisees' dinner invitations, we remember more what Jesus says in response, how he calls Herod "that fox," and how he mourns for Jerusalem (Luke 13:31-35). In our selective memory, we forget that some Pharisees did not want Jesus to die. We do not know what they risked in order to warn him, but it adds a new dimension to the "Pharisees plotting against Jesus" stereotype with which many of us grew up.

In the Gospel of John, which often makes scathing attacks on Pharisees and Jewish leaders, we find two accounts that run counter to the stereotype. One involves Nicodemus, a Pharisee and "a leader." Most people are familiar with the account in John 3, where Jesus teaches Nicodemus the meaning of becoming "born again." Again we see a Pharisee who earnestly wishes to learn from Jesus and hear what he has to say.

Nicodemus also speaks up for Jesus at some personal risk when the temple police fail to arrest Jesus as instructed by the chief priests and Pharisees. In John 7:51, he says, "Our law does not judge people without first giving them a hearing to find out what they are doing, does it?" The aristocratic Jews of Jerusalem then imply that Nicodemus might himself be just another peasant from Galilee.

In John 19:38-42, we read of how Nicodemus brings expensive spices with which to prepare Jesus' corpse. He assists Joseph of Arimathea, another member of the religious establishment, to ensure that Jesus' corpse has a proper burial.

The other example in John that shows Pharisees in a positive light appears within a passage that also portrays them negatively. When Jesus heals the man born blind, the people bring him before the Pharisees. Because Jesus healed the man on the Sabbath, some of the Pharisees say, "This man is not from God, for he does not observe the sabbath." In the second half of John 9:16 we read, "But *others* said, 'How can a man who is a sinner perform such signs?' *And they were divided*" (italics added). In other words, at least some of the Pharisees present understand that something has happened which transcends their understanding of the law of Moses. They know they have witnessed a miracle of God's grace and do not wish to nitpick about the rules of Sabbath observance.

Pharisees and Paul

When we move ahead in time to the ministry of Paul, we receive a much different picture of the Pharisees. He only mentions the term once in his letters—the earliest written documents of the New Testament. Consider Philippians 3:4b-7:

> If anyone else has reason to be confident in the flesh, I have more: circumcised on the eighth day, a member of the people of Israel, of the tribe of Benjamin, a Hebrew born of Hebrews; as to the law, a Pharisee; as to zeal, a persecutor of the church; as to righteousness under the law, blameless. *Yet whatever gains I had,* these I have come to regard as loss because of Christ. (italics added)

Notice that Paul does *not* say, "I used to be a Pharisee and then I realized it was a bad thing to be a Pharisee and became a Christian."

Paul clearly regards being a Pharisee as a positive thing—so positive that he might feel temptation to take pride in his status as someone who rigorously upholds the law. But Christ has become so important in his life that he regards his former status as nothing.

In the book of Acts, where references to Pharisees mostly have a positive element, we find that Paul used his status as a Pharisee several times to his advantage. When he is later brought before the Sanhedrin after a disturbance in the temple, he calls out to the Pharisees on the council, identifying himself with them, both because of his upbringing and because of his belief in the resurrection of the dead. Certain Pharisees on the council stand up for Paul and say they find nothing wrong with him. Recognizing the risk of convicting a true follower of God, they ask, "What if a spirit or an angel has spoken to him?" Since the Sadducees do not believe in resurrection of the dead, whether in the form of angels or spirits,[4] this remark causes an already ugly situation to become violent. The Roman tribune takes Paul away to ensure his physical safety (Acts 23:1-10.)

When Paul, still a prisoner, comes before Herod Agrippa, he defends his status as not only a Jew, but a Jew who has had a strict upbringing in the faith—a Jew, in fact, who is a Pharisee (Acts 26:5-8).

A cynic might point out that Paul fell back on his Roman citizenship when he found it useful to do so and likewise used his Judaism to its full advantage (Acts 22:25-29; and references above). Again, however, we need to remember that nowhere did Paul say, "I used to be a Jew," or "I used to be a Pharisee." Instead, he adopted the additional faith stance of the Christians and set out to convert the Gentiles.

Acts 15:5 shows that Pharisees could belong to the Christian church as well (cf. 11:2). Just as many Christians blip over the fact of Pharisees offering hospitality to Jesus to focus on his condemnation of them, they have blipped over another fact to focus on the Pharisees' legalism: the book of Acts says that *some Pharisees were Christians.*

The issue of whether Gentile believers had to conform to Jewish regulations caused great controversy in the early church. Many of Paul's writings stemmed from this issue, and it caused a rift between him and Peter (Gal. 2:9-14). It is not surprising that the Christian Pharisees, brought up to serve God rigorously in normal day-to-day tasks of living, should want Jewish rituals upheld. They stuck by ancestral traditions. Better safe than sorry. We do them a disservice, however, when we forget that these "believers who belonged to the sect of the Pharisees" committed themselves to Christ, just as Paul and the apostles had (Acts 15:5). We should also consider that most Jews despised Gentiles as unclean. The Christian Pharisees seemed able to accept Gentiles as fellow Christians—provided that they conformed to become God's chosen people.

Before we leave the book of Acts, we should take note of another positive reference to Pharisees. When certain members of the Sanhedrin wished to kill Peter and his fellow apostles because of what they did in the name of Christ, a Pharisee named Gamaliel probably saved their lives by a logical observation. He noted that in the past other people had claimed to have special revelations from God and they had perished. Then he proposed that if the faith of Peter and the other disciples stemmed from human origins, they would fail in their mission as had other religious fanatics. If, however, their revelation did come from God, the religious leaders would not be able to stop them. Indeed, they would feel awkward when they realized they had been fighting God! (Acts 5:33-39).

The Pharisees as Questioners

A number of passages concerning the Pharisees in the New Testament show them in neither a negative nor positive light. Many make their appearance in the Gospel narratives because they honestly wanted to know what this Jesus guy was all about. He had said some radical things, and his actions did not seem consistent with this authority as a teacher.

Examine Matthew 9:1-13. We have discussed earlier in the chapter the parallel account in Luke 5 of the healing of the paralyzed man. Immediately following both accounts, we read that Jesus met a tax collector. Jesus then proceeds to eat with many tax collectors and assorted sinners.

Look at the situation from the perspective of the Pharisees involved. They have witnessed or heard of Jesus healing a paralyzed man. They know he is no ordinary preacher. He has said that he has the authority to forgive sins and has demonstrated this authority through the miraculous healing. Next he invites a tax collector to follow him as a disciple. Then he has dinner with many tax collectors and other people with bad reputations.

To appreciate the dilemma of the well-intentioned Pharisee at this point, we need to understand a little more about tax collectors. The Pharisees did not dislike them only for reasons of religious bigotry. Every Jew despised tax collectors. People today complain of tax burdens, but the situation in first-century Palestine was much worse. In addition to the tithes the Jews owed to the temple, they had to give up to one quarter of their harvest to the Roman government and owed a portion to Herod and the later Roman procurators as well.

These taxes caused significant hardship for the people of Palestine. It is estimated that they paid between one half and two-thirds of all they produced in taxes and additional rents to large land owners.[5] Remember that they received no medical care, education, or social services in return for their taxes as we do.

The Jews who collected their money had literally "sold

out" to the Romans, who gave the office of tax collector to the highest bidder. On top of that, they added a surcharge for their services as tax collectors that further impoverished the working poor of Palestine.[6] Under Jewish law, a sinner who wished to repent had to make restitution to all against whom he or she had committed an injustice. Since a tax collector could not possibly remember all the people he had defrauded, he had no way of genuinely repenting.[7]

Thus Jesus did not just eat with average sinners. He ate with flunkies of the Roman government who had impoverished many people. To put the enormity of this event into a contemporary perspective, think of Jesus going to El Salvador and choosing to eat with officers of the military regime instead of those who have served the Salvadoran people at great personal risk.

Perhaps we might forgive the Pharisees for asking Jesus' disciples, "Why does your teacher eat with tax collectors and sinners?" How could someone who had demonstrated such holy authority eat with such vile company immediately afterward?

There are references in the Gospels to the Pharisees "testing" Jesus with hard questions.[8] But again, when we look at the situation from their standpoint, we can sympathize to some extent with their goals. If someone came to us claiming to have special knowledge of God, we would want to ask some questions ourselves. We would not pledge our loyalty lightly. We might well be suspicious of those making such claims of authority and go out of our way to trip them up.

The fact that the Pharisees asked questions of Jesus does not discredit them, even if they received rebukes from him in response. As a people who treasured knowledge of God and hoped for a Messiah, it is only natural that they tried to pump Jesus with as many questions as they could. They took him seriously enough to be in dialogue with him.

Differences Between the Gospels

Have you noticed that a lot of the passages that show Pharisees in a positive light are from Luke and Acts, and that many of the negative references come from Matthew? Because each of the Gospels was written to minister to the young Christian churches from different places and/or different generations, each has a unique perspective on the relationship between Christianity and Judaism.

The Gospel of Mark

Matthew, Mark, and Luke are called the *synoptic Gospels* because they "see together." The Synoptics share many of the same stories and traditions that the disciples and other early Christians had passed down orally about Jesus Christ. Because Matthew and Luke seem to borrow much of their material from Mark, most scholars believe that Mark is the oldest of the three Synoptics. Of all the Gospels, Mark has the least to say about the Pharisees. With one exception, 12:13, he places the encounters that Jesus has with the Pharisees in Galilee.

Reading the book of Mark apart from the other Gospels would leave one with a largely negative impression of the Pharisees. In three instances he refers to them setting out to "test" or "trap" Jesus.[9] They, their behavior, and their beliefs seem to serve as a contrast to what Jesus expected of his followers.[10] The Pharisees, however, play no role in Jesus' arrest or execution as described in Mark 14:1—15:39.

The Gospel of Matthew

Matthew mentions the Pharisees the most often and the most critically. In chapter 23, we find a virulent attack on the Pharisees—harsher than anything found in the other three Gospels. Jesus states explicitly in 21:42-46 that the kingdom of God will be taken away from them and the other members of the Jewish establishment and given to those who more truly follow in God's ways. Matthew hints that the Pharisees, if not involved in Jesus' actual arrest, did arrange to place a guard at the tomb to foil any disciples' attempt to steal the body and claim that Jesus had risen from the dead (Matt. 27:62-66).

The hostility in Matthew may reflect a growing tension between the Christian church, which considered itself a part of Judaism for much of the first century, and the Jewish establishment. The Gospel of Matthew may have comforted Christian Jews, by telling them that they were the ones who truly constituted the kingdom of God, not the people who rejected them.

The Gospel of Luke

You may have noticed in this chapter that many of the positive depictions of Pharisees appear in Luke. Since most scholars agree that the author of Luke also wrote the book of Acts, it is tempting to generalize and say Luke-Acts is a "gentler" Gospel than Matthew or Mark. However, Luke 11:37—12:1 roughly parallels the hostile "woes" passage of Matthew 23. Furthermore, Luke is the only one of the four Gospels in which Jesus accuses the Pharisees of being lovers of money and the only one to contain the parable of the Pharisee and the tax collector (18:9-14).

On the other hand, in parallel stories shared with Mark and Matthew that sketch the Pharisees negatively, Luke omits naming them and instead refers to the "villains" as scribes, lawyers, "crowds," or "others."[11] Luke tells of how certain Pharisees came to warn Jesus of Herod's intention to kill him and how others invited him to dinner.[12]

How do we reconcile the negative and positive portrayals of Pharisees in Luke-Acts? Again, we need to place it in the context of the early church and the Jewish-Christian conflict. Clearly Luke does not regard the Pharisees as the same sort of threat that Matthew does.[13] Along with Mark, he seems to value them in part as a contrast to Jesus' teachings. Hence, the negative portrayals.

More importantly, however, Luke-Acts uses the Pharisees to add legitimacy to Gentile Christianity. Admission of Gentiles into Christianity was a source of conflict in the early church. Luke-Acts, by showing some Pharisees as having received the good news of Jesus Christ, demonstrates that there is nothing inherently "un-Jewish" about Christianity. Luke, a Gentile himself, wanted to show that the kingdom of God was inclusive rather than exclusive.[14]

The Gospel of John

The Gospel of John is a special case. It developed from a different tradition than the Synoptics and forms a comprehensive theology in its own style. John's negative references to Pharisees are less striking to the reader than the way he talks of Jews in general, meaning Jewish leaders.[15] It is hard to determine whether John used the two terms interchangeably. The Pharisees have considerably more power in John than they do in the other three Gospels, including the power (with the chief priests) to order Jesus' arrest (7:32; 11:57).

As with Matthew, the author of the Gospel of John speaks to a situation within the early church. Christian and non-Christian Jews had come into bitter conflict with each other, and evidently the leaders of the synagogues had begun to expel Jews who professed a belief in Christ (John 9:22; 12:42; 16:2). Unlike Matthew, which demonstrates a bitterness rooted in an ongoing struggle, John seems to mark the point at which Christianity and Judaism split and went in separate directions.[16]

For Discussion

1. Who are the people of the religious establishment today? Which ones most affect your life?

2. Is there an issue in the church today that is as divisive as the issue of circumcision was to the early church? What issues have divided your denomination in particular?

3. Refer again to the story of Paulina Yoder that opens this chapter. Imagine that this took place before modern communication devices. The New Wineskins churches, after flourishing for a couple decades, decide to write a history of Paulina's life and teachings. How might the account written by her followers in South America differ from the one put out by the mission board in North America? Suppose the New Wineskins communities in Oregon faced governmental persecution. Perhaps a Spanish-reading pastor translated the original history, adding editorial comments to minister to the specific needs of the churches in Oregon and British Columbia. What changes might he make?

4

Negative Accounts of Pharisees in the Gospels

The Prodigal Son: A Sequel

After their father died, the two brothers tried to get along, but the tension between them never quite went away. The older brother was not unwilling to share his portion of the inheritance with the brother who had squandered his own share. But, well, he thought his younger brother could have shown him a little more respect, maybe even some gratitude.

Instead, this brother took his position on the family farm for granted. He acted as though he had the same authority asserted by the older brother in managing the property. The older brother felt especially infuriated by the way the younger brother would say, "Well, my father would have wanted us to do it this way."

Had he forgotten how his older brother had stayed behind to help and support his father when he went to the city and squandered his fortune on fast living? The older brother did not need to hear from the younger brother what his father would have thought. He had stuck by his father through good times and bad. Now his younger brother acted as though he had every bit as much right to run the family farm as he did.

The tension eventually exploded into some nasty fights. Some of the servants and other members of the household sided with the older brother. They regarded him as a responsible and reliable person and believed that the younger brother did not defer to him as he should.

Other servants and members of the household sided with the younger brother. They believed he was more a man like his father in management of the farm. He was not as stern or judgmental as his older brother. And they were tired of the older brother throwing into the younger one's face that reckless episode of his youth. Why couldn't the older brother forgive the younger and get on with his life?

Emotions mounted until people and servants of the household began to commit acts of violence against each other. Eventually, the older brother threw the younger brother and his supporters off the land. He took care to change the locks on the doors lest they decide to sneak back by night.

• • •

In the early church, certain Christians wrote *apologies*, works that served to defend the Christian church against persecutors, critics, and heretics. By this point you may wonder whether this book will serve as an apology for the Pharisees. It won't.

The last chapter highlighted some often overlooked passages that present the Pharisees in a positive or at least neutral light. We will have a lopsided understanding of the Pharisees, however, if we do not include the many negative or even hostile references to them in the New Testament.

In this chapter we will explore in more depth passages which present the Pharisees in an unfavorable light. We will look first at a parable from Luke 18:9-14 referred to in the opening chapter. Then we will examine the most protracted and hostile polemic against the Pharisees found in the New Testament, Matthew 23:1-36.

The Pharisee and the Tax Collector

> Luke 18:[9]He also told this parable to some who trusted in themselves that they were righteous and regarded others with contempt: [10]"Two men went up to the temple to pray, one a Pharisee and the other a tax collector. [11]The Pharisee, standing by himself, was praying thus, 'God, I thank you that I am not like other people: thieves, rogues, adulterers, or even like this tax collector. [12]I fast twice a week; I give a tenth of all my income.' [13]But the tax collector, standing far off, would not even look up to heaven, but was beating his breast and saying, 'God, be merciful to me, a sinner!' [14]I tell you, this man went down to his home justified rather than the other; for all who exalt themselves will be humbled, but all who humble themselves will be exalted."

As mentioned in the last chapter, the Gospel of Luke uses Pharisees as a foil to show that the kingdom of God is not exclusive but open to all who repent. Luke 18:9-14 furthers this theme by demonstrating that the Pharisee, who thinks he has won God's favor by his acts of piety, has not done what it takes to enter the kingdom. The tax collector, who may never have done a pious deed in his life, has won admittance by the acknowledgment of his unworthiness.

When Jesus told the story of the good Samaritan in Luke 10:30-37 and asked his listeners who proved to be a neighbor to the man who had been attacked, they would have found the answer obvious. Many Jews despised the Samaritans for their mixed-race heritage and their rejection of the Jerusalem temple. Yet in spite of the longstanding feud, they could not deny that the Samaritan alone of the travelers on that road had shown mercy to the robbery victim.

Suppose Jesus had left off the last line of the parable of the Pharisee and the tax collector and asked, "Now who do you think the truly righteous one was?" His listeners would not have found the answer as obvious as the one for the parable of the good Samaritan. A first-century prayer recorded in the Talmud runs as follows:

> I thank thee, O Lord my God, that thou has given me my lot with those who sit in the seat of learning and not with those who sit at the street-corners; for I am early to work, and they are early to work; I am early to work on the words of the Torah, and they are early to work on things of no moment. I weary myself and they weary themselves; I weary myself and profit thereby, while they worry themselves to no profit. I run and they run; I run towards the life of the Age to Come and they run towards the well of the pit. (b. Ber. 28b)[1]

To our modern eyes, the prayer of the Pharisee and the prayer from the Talmud seem obviously self-righteous. But look closer at the passage in Luke. The Pharisee does not ask God for anything. His prayer is a prayer of thanksgiving. He feels truly grateful that he does not have the misfortune to be in the same circumstances as thieves, rogues, adulterers, and tax collectors.

How many of us, when hearing of a friend's cancer or an acquaintance's children causing her misery, do not breathe a quick prayer of thanks that we do not find ourselves in the same circumstances? And what fault can we find with the thanksgiving in the Talmudic prayer for the opportunity to study God's Word?

The law of Moses requires a regular fast only on Yom Kippur, the Day of Atonement, in penitence. This Pharisee fasts twice a week to intercede with God for the sins of his people. When we consider the arid climate of Palestine, we can appreciate the sacrifice involved if he abstains not only from food but also from water. The Law requires that people tithe 10 percent of only grain, wine, and oil; the Pharisee tithes 10 percent of everything he earns, grows, or buys to ensure that God will get his due.[2] Robert Capon, in a sermon on this parable, writes, "If you know where to find a dozen or two such upstanding citizens, I know several parishes that will accept delivery of them, no questions asked."[3]

It is difficult to describe to the average North American churchgoer the loathing and disgust with which the average upright Jewish citizen regarded tax collectors. The resentment some people feel for the IRS or Revenue Canada does not even come close to the loathing felt for tax collectors in Palestine at that time (see above, chapter 3). We might compare it to our own attitude toward a drug dealer or a pimp (see above, chapter 1).

Capon characterizes the tax collector in more colorful terms. He is

> the worst kind of crook: a legal one, a big operator, a mafia-style enforcer working for the Roman government on a nifty franchise that lets him collect—from his fellow Jews, mind you . . . all the money he can bleed out of them, provided only he pays the authorities an agreed flat fee. . . . He is a fat cat who drives a stretch limo, drinks nothing but Chivas Regal and never shows up at a party without at least two $500-a-night call girls in tow.[4]

Comparing the average Pharisee unfavorably with a tax collector would have astonished Jesus' listeners. In fact, had he compared an illiterate Jewish peasant with the tax collector, people might have felt shocked all the same. Tax collectors consorted with Gentiles, which made them unclean. In addition, they aided Gentiles in oppressing the

Jews of Palestine. They added to the already crushing tax burden imposed on the Jews by the Romans.

The tax collector in the parable, even if he gave up his livelihood the next day, would never become truly "clean" again in the estimation of the Pharisees. It would be almost impossible for him to make reparation to the countless people he had defrauded. Thus this tax collector beat his chest as a token of his despair. He had no right to expect God to forgive him. The fact that he stood "far off" shows that he doubted his right to soil God's holy temple with his presence.

Yet in the end, Jesus said that this vile sinner had more right to enter the kingdom of God than did the Pharisee who had done everything right to ensure his salvation. Jesus' astonishing good news was that the kingdom of God shattered the well-drawn social and religious boundaries of the first century. It could accommodate Samaritans, Gentiles, sinners, and, yes, Pharisees who acknowledged that they had no hope of making everything "just right." God wanted all to repent and welcomed lovingly those who did.

Jesus Denouncing the Scribes and Pharisees

Matthew 23 occupies the same place in the book of Matthew that Mark 12:38-40 does in the book of Mark. In both cases, the condemnation of scribes and Pharisees comes after a controversy with them over the identity of the son of David. The passage in Matthew, however, becomes a prolonged tirade with almost vicious overtones.

Why? Place yourself again in the position of members of the early Christian church, who wanted to remain in fellowship with their Jewish friends and relations. The Jews of Palestine, bitter over the Roman occupation and destruction of Jerusalem, were not in a mood to humor a movement that seemed to eschew Jewish customs and welcome Gentiles. The anger in Matthew 23 reflects the emotions of a people persecuted for their beliefs and rejected by those closest to them in belief.

Hypocritical Pharisees

> Matthew 23:[1]Jesus said to the crowds and to his disciples, [2]The scribes and the Pharisees sit on Moses' seat; [3]therefore, do whatever they teach you and follow it; but do not do as they do, for they do not practice what they teach.

Sunday school children learn early to associate hypocrisy with the Pharisees. Notice, however, that Jesus does not criticize *what* the Pharisees teach in these verses, nor does Jesus say that they should not occupy "Moses' seat" (probably a chair in which the most distinguished scholar of the community sat in the synagogue while teaching). Indeed, he implies that because the Pharisees and scribes have a place of honor in the synagogue, people should heed their teachings.

Matthew mentions the *scribes* more than any of the other Gospel writers, both by themselves and as companions of the Pharisees.[5] As with all the other religious and sociological groups in first-century Palestine, we have limited information available to us. The New Testament associates the scribes with Pharisees, prophets, elders, chief priests, and rulers. From the three times they are mentioned in Acts (4:5; 6:12; 23:9), it appears that some of them sat on the Sanhedrin.

The standing that scribes had in the community could vary. Some worked for the Jewish government and the temple, preserving sacred literature and advising the chief priests. Others served as copyists and letter writers for the illiterate in small villages. The scribes were authoritative teachers of Jewish law and custom. In Jewish tradition, the rabbis later took over the religious duties of the scribes.[6]

In affirming the teachings of the scribes and the Pharisees, the Gospel of Matthew may have provided reassurance to Jewish Christians of the first century that they had not completely broken with the faith of their ancestors.[7]

It is interesting to note that portions of the Dead Sea Scrolls also accuse the Pharisees of hypocrisy, as do portions of the Talmud.[8] Because they set high standards for themselves in religious and moral behavior, they risked falling short of these standards more than other Jewish groups did.

Heartless Pharisees

Matthew 23:[4]They tie up heavy burdens, hard to bear, and lay them on the shoulders of others; but they themselves are unwilling to lift a finger to move them.

Luke 11:[46]Woe also to you lawyers! For you load people with burdens hard to bear, and you yourselves do not lift a finger to ease them.

The passage suggests the image of a yoke laid across a person's shoulders in order to help him or her to bear burdens, such as a heavy bucket on each side. In this case, the "bucket" holds the collection of laws that evolved in oral tradition.

In the Talmud, one of the most important pieces of oral tradition is, "Be deliberate in judgment, raise up many disciples, and make a fence around the Law."[9] In order to save people from transgressing one of the commandments, Jewish oral tradition developed regulations—or fences—that made it easier for people to keep the commandments.

One example of observing the fence around the Law would be that of the kosher diet that many contemporary Jews still keep. In Exodus 23:19 and 34:26 we find a command not to boil a goat kid in its mother's milk. Certain documents from the ancient Canaanite city of Ugarit speak of this practice as part of the ritual of sacrifice to Canaanite gods.[10] The Law in Exodus, then, essentially was intended to keep Israelites from pagan religious practices.

Today, those people who keep a kosher kitchen have separate dishes for serving dairy products and meat products. They run no risk of violating the commandment in Exodus, because they never allow meat products or dairy products to touch each other.

Lest you think that doing so takes the commandment in Exodus to the extreme, remember that most secular laws operate on the same principle. Municipalities set speed limits not because it is inherently unsafe for a person to travel a hundred miles an hour, but because doing so makes it more likely that he or she will have an accident. Christians may choose not to drink alcohol or dance—not because the Bible forbids these activities, but because engaging in them may make it more likely that they will do something that does break a commandment.

The book *Growing Up Born Again* illustrates this principle of a Christian hedge in its fictional youth sermon on sex and dating:

> "How far can you go? How far is too far?". . . .
> "That's like asking, 'How long can I hold my hand in a flame without getting burned?' And that's *not* the question you should be asking! You *should* be asking the question, 'How far from the flame should I stay?' "[11]

Those who developed the regulations and laws that constituted the "hedge around the Torah" did not intend them to become burdensome. They designed them to be helpful, to act as a safety net or buffer zone for people who earnestly wished to follow God's Law but tripped up sometimes. In time, however, people began to focus more on the fence than on the Law, and the numerous regulations that comprised the fence became increasing difficult for people to keep.

In saying, *"They themselves are unwilling to lift a finger to move them,"* Jesus could mean that the Pharisees, after saddling bewildered converts with a dizzying array of regulations and rules they must keep, did nothing to help these people carry their new and unwieldy burden. A less likely interpretation would be that the Pharisees sought to evade the responsibilities they laid on others.

Notice that the parallel passage in Luke does not mention Pharisees at all but *lawyers*. Luke mentions lawyers much more often than the other Gospel writers.[12] We should not confuse them with contemporary attorneys but think of them instead as part of the religious establishment, along with Pharisees, Sadducees, priests, and scribes, with which Jesus clashed. In the time and place where the Gospel of Luke achieved final written form, lawyers, more than scribes, may have functioned as experts on religious Law.[13]

As such, their appearance in this passage seems especially appropriate. Unlike the "easy" yoke of Jesus (Matt. 11:30), the yoke fashioned by the experts on the Law was cumbersome and made following God's Law more difficult for those who bore it.

Show-off Pharisees

Matthew 23:[5]They do all their deeds to be seen by others; for they make their phylacteries broad and their fringes long. [6]They love to have the place of honor at banquets and the

Mark 12:[38]Beware of the scribes, who like to walk around in long robes, and to be greeted with respect in the marketplaces, [39]and to have the best seats in the synagogues and places of

Luke 11:[43]Woe to you Pharisees! For you love to have the seat of honor in the synagogues and to be greeted with respect in the marketplaces.

best seats in the synagogues, [7]and to be greeted with respect in the marketplaces, and to have people call them rabbi.

honor at banquets!

The Pharisees were diligent in carrying out the commands of Deuteronomy 6:4-9, which says,

> Hear O Israel: The Lord is our God, the Lord alone. You shall love the Lord your God with all your heart, and with all your soul, and with all your might. Keep these words that I am commanding you today in your heart. Recite them to your children and talk about them when you are at home and when you are away, when you lie down and when you rise. Bind them as a sign on your hand, fix them as an emblem on your forehead, and write them on the doorposts of your house and on your gates.

For centuries, observant Jews have taken this commandment literally and worn *phylacteries* while praying. Each phylactery is a leather case containing strips of vellum on which were written certain Scriptures (Exod. 13:1-10, 11-16; Deut. 6:4-9, 11:13-21).[14] One case is then bound to the forehead and the other to the left arm. The idea behind phylacteries is that God's words are continually present in the mind of the believer and in the believer's actions (symbolized by the forehead and the arm).

Oral tradition does not specify what size the phylacteries ought to be, but it is possible that some men wore ostentatiously large ones. Jesus' criticism here probably reflects the same criticism he made in Matthew 6:5-6 of those who pray aloud on the street corners.

The significance of the fringes can be found in Numbers 15:38-39:

> Speak to the Israelites, and tell them to make fringes on the corners of their garments throughout their generations and to put a blue cord on the fringe at each corner. You have the fringe so that, when you see it, you will remember all the commandments of the Lord and do them, and not follow the lust of your own heart and your own eyes.

In both the case of the phylacteries and the fringes, then, we see that the motives for wearing them were good—even commanded by God. But some people perverted the motives for wearing them in order to appear holy to others. They may even have had crasser motives, such as drawing people's attention to themselves in the marketplaces, at banquets, or on the street.

Other ways of impressing people with their religiosity included taking the seats of honor in the synagogue. We do not have any primary sources that detail seating arrangements in first-century synagogues, but the practice of seating more "important" people in the best seats has occurred frequently in church history. At one time it was common in many mainstream churches for the "most important" members of the congregation to occupy (and even pay for) the best pews in the sanctuary. The Free Methodist Church in the nineteenth century took its name because it advocated freedom for slaves, freedom from oaths, and free seating in their churches "so that all might hear the gospel."[15]

Notice that Mark accuses "scribes" instead of Pharisees in the parallel passage in 12:38-39. Luke 11:43 mentions Pharisees specifically, but differentiates them from the lawyers in 11:46. In Luke's view it is the Pharisees who want to show off and curry favor, but it is the lawyers who oppress people with the Law.

In contrast to those who show off and covet honor, Jesus describes how believers should behave.

Matthew 23:[8]But you are not to be called rabbi, for you have one teacher, and you are all students. [9]And call no one your father on earth, for you have one Father—the one in heaven. [10]Nor are you to be called instructors, for you have one instructor, the Messiah.

The term *rabbi* was just coming into use in the first century. It comes from a root word meaning "great." In time, Judaism came to apply the word almost exclusively to scholars and teachers. We know that some people in the early church did serve as teachers, and Jesus probably did not mean that teachers had no place in the Christian community. Rather, Jesus deplored any word that ranked one person above another. All believers, both learned and ignorant, ultimately were students of the Messiah, their "instructor."

In a patriarchal society, the title *father* could confer distinction on certain men—a sort of master-slave relationship. (It could also refer to the patriarchs, Abraham, Isaac, and Jacob.) Jesus wanted his followers to know that they should relate to each other as brothers and sisters. The more learned, "important" people should not treat the less learned and less important in a paternalistic manner.

Matthew 23:[11]The greatest among you will be your servant. [12]All who exalt themselves will be humbled, and all who humble themselves will be exalted.

Luke14:[11]For all who exalt themselves will be humbled, and those who humble themselves will be exalted.

The word translated here as "servant" is the Greek word *diakonos.* The true leaders of the fledgling church hungered to serve—as *deacons*, or *ministers,* as the Latin says. In Matthew 23:12, we find echoes from the story of the Pharisee and the Tax Collector. In the context of Matthew, the foundation of a new humility and a new exaltation will take place in the future, after the kingdom has come.

First Woe: Exclusiveness of the Pharisees

Matthew 23:[13]But woe to you, scribes and Pharisees, hypocrites! For you lock people out of the kingdom of heaven. For you do not go in yourselves, and when others are going in, you stop them.

Luke 11:[52]Woe to you lawyers! For you have taken away the key of knowledge; you did not enter yourselves, and you hindered those who were entering.

In the parallel passage in Luke, this "woe" serves as the climax of the diatribe in 11:37-52. Note again that Luke blames lawyers rather than the Pharisees.

In keeping with their desire to follow the Law strictly in their everyday living, some Pharisees shut out those who did not conform to their regulations.[16] Jesus spoke scornfully of this exclusiveness, saying that the regulated community from which they wished to exclude people would not guarantee them the kingdom of heaven.

This passage may have spoken to the Matthean community as Jewish and Gentile Christians sought to define themselves. We know that some Jewish Christians did not fellowship with Gentiles who had not undergone the rites of circumcision (Gal. 2:11-14; Acts 15:1-5; cf. Rom. 14). This passage spoke against such exclusiveness.[17]

Second Woe: Pharisees and Their Converts

Matthew 23:[15]Woe to you, scribes and Pharisees, hypocrites! For you cross sea and land to make a single convert, and you make the new convert twice as much a child of hell as yourselves.

In first-century Judaism, converts seemed to be welcomed.[18] The Talmud, in recording disputes between the school of Hillel and the school of Shammai portray Hillel as a teacher who wished to make Judaism accessible to non-Jews.[19] Conversion to Judaism involved baptism, circumcision, and making an offering in the temple. These were called "converts" or "proselytes" (cf. Acts 2:10; 6:5; 13:43). Judaism also made room for "sympathizers" who attended the synagogue worship service, acknowledged the one God, and observed the Sabbath and certain Jewish dietary laws.[20]

As one might expect, the Pharisees in Palestine held a stricter view of what it meant to convert to Judaism. Keeping in mind the early Christian community for whom the Gospel of Matthew was written, we also might hear echoes of warning for the evangelistic practices of the early Jewish Christians.

In a contemporary context, we often observe that new converts to a religion sometimes behave more aggressively and may become more bigoted than people who converted them. By giving new converts a load of minor regulations upon which they could zealously obsess, some Pharisees may have caused the convert to miss the heart of what their religion meant.[21]

Third Woe: Blind Guides, Who Allow Oaths

> Matthew 23:[16]Woe to you, blind guides, who say, "Whoever swears by the sanctuary is bound by nothing, but whoever swears by the gold of the sanctuary is bound by the oath." [17]You blind fools! For which is greater, the gold or the sanctuary that has made the gold sacred? [18]And you say, "Whoever swears by the altar is bound by nothing, but whoever swears by the gift that is on the altar is bound by the oath." [19]How blind you are! For which is greater, the gift or the altar that makes the gift sacred? [20]So whoever swears by the altar, swears by it and by everything on it;

> [21]and whoever swears by the sanctuary, swears by it and by the one who dwells in it; [22]and whoever swears by heaven, swears by the throne of God and by the one who is seated upon it.

We know from Matthew 5:33-37 that Jesus cut through all the societal regulations regarding oath-taking. Since the swearing of oaths implied that ordinarily the oath-takers spoke falsely, Jesus wanted to do away with them altogether. His followers had the obligation to speak the truth at all times.

Since people in Hellenistic societies had become habitual oath-takers, Jewish religious leaders developed regulations in their oral tradition to keep them from referring to the sacred items in the temple carelessly.[22] As with the other regulations designed to help people remain faithful to the Law, those regarding oath-taking could become a burden rather than an asset and get in the way of understanding the spirit of the Law.

Fourth Woe: Pharisees, Tithing, Gnat-picking

Matthew 23:[23]Woe to you, scribes and Pharisees, hypocrites! For you tithe mint, dill, and cummin, and have neglected the weightier matters of the law: justice and mercy and faith. It is these you ought to have practiced without neglecting the others. [24]You blind guides! You strain out a gnat but swallow a camel!

Luke 11:[42]But woe to you Pharisees! For you tithe mint and rue and herbs of all kinds, and neglect justice and the love of God; it is these you ought to have practiced, without neglecting the others.

We should view verses 23 and 24 as a continuum with verses 25-27. The Pharisees believed that any food which had not had a portion tithed to the temple was unclean, just as much as if it were an unclean animal, or eaten on unclean dishes.[23]

Deuteronomy 14:22-23 describes how God's faithful should tithe grain, wine, and oil. The Talmud records how the rabbis built their "hedge around the Law" by ensuring that all foodstuffs be tithed, including dill and cumin.[24] The religious establishment in first-century Palestine required tithing, although for different reasons. Since the temple's income came from these tithes, the Sadducees and priests demanded scrupulous observance of this religious "tax" from faithful Jews (already carrying an enormous tax burden; see chapter 3, above). As mentioned before, the Pharisees' determination to tithe stemmed from their emphasis on ritual purity in everyday aspects of their lives.[25]

Jesus did not object to the scribes and Pharisees tithing negligible amounts of kitchen herbs. He objected first to their belief that doing so made them "holier" people. Second, he criticized the tunnel vision that allowed them to concentrate acutely on tithing food but shut out the far greater issues of justice, mercy, and faith—which the Law was to uphold (cf. Mic. 6:6-8). Indeed, Jesus specifically tells the Pharisees that they need to focus on the "weightier matters of the law . . . *without neglecting the others*" (italics added), meaning other matters of the Law such as tithing. In short, Jesus wants believers to attend to justice, mercy, and faith. If, while focusing on these matters, they trip up on some of the many tithing regulations, well, better that than the other way around.

Leviticus 11:4-7 and Deuteronomy 14:7-8 specifically forbid the consumption of camels (as well as hares and rock badgers) because they do not have divided hoofs. From Leviticus 11:20-23, we can determine that gnats do not make the cut as "kosher" insects (though certain varieties of grasshoppers do). The biting irony of the verse is clear. In their zeal for ritual purity, the Pharisees strain out any little gnat that might accidentally fall into their wine, but they neglect to notice that they commit far bigger (camel-sized) violations of the Law. In fact, it is the "gnat-picking" itself that makes them blind to these violations.

Fifth Woe: Pharisees and Dishwashing

Matthew 23:[25]Woe to you, scribes and Pharisees, hypocrites! For you clean the outside of the cup and of the plate, but inside they are full of greed and self-indulgence. [26]You blind Pharisee! First clean the inside of the cup, so that the outside also may become clean.

Luke 11:[37]While he was speaking, a Pharisee invited him to dine with him; so he went in and took his place at the table. [38]The Pharisee was amazed to see that he did not first wash before dinner. [39]Then the Lord said to him, Now you Pharisees clean the outside of the cup and of the dish, but inside you are full of greed and wickedness. [40]You fools! Did not the one who made the outside make the inside also? [41]So give for alms those things that are within; and see, everything will be clean for you.

As Jesus continues to criticize the ritual purity which blinds the Pharisees to the deeper obligations that the Law requires of them, he addresses the ceremonies involved in making their meals acceptable and holy.

With our modern standards of hygiene, we do not find anything particularly objectionable in the Pharisees insisting on washing hands before a meal, nor in washing their dishes. In saying that the Pharisees did not wash the inside of their cups and dishes, Jesus exaggerates for effect. The Pharisees most certainly did wash the inside of their dishes. The importance of clean dishes acquired immense proportions for the Pharisees. Some of the earliest rabbinical judgments recorded in the Talmud had to do with the inherent uncleanness of glassware and metalware from Gentile nations.[26]

If a mouse ran across a plate or a bone fell into a cup during a meal, those utensils became ritually unclean.[27] In the still unpublished Halakhic Letter (4QMMT) of the Dead Sea Scrolls, we find a criticism of the Pharisees as people who believed that, when something was poured from a clean vessel into a ritually unclean vessel, the unclean one did not contaminate the clean one. (The community at the Dead Sea believed the impurities could travel from the unclean vessel upwards against the stream and contaminate the clean one.)[28]

Jesus did not object to how the Pharisees cleaned their dishes any more than he objected to their tithing or keeping kosher food regulations. Jesus objected to people making an outward presentation of holiness to the neglect of the inner person. It was not the inside of their cups that needed cleaning, it was their hearts.

Sixth Woe: Pharisees and External Righteousness

Matthew 23:[27]Woe to you, scribes and Pharisees, hypocrites! For you are like whitewashed tombs, which on the outside look beautiful, but inside they are full of the bones of the dead and of all kinds of filth. [28]So you also on the outside look righteous to others, but inside you are full of hypocrisy and lawlessness.

Luke 11:44 Woe to you [Pharisees]! For you are like unmarked graves, and people walk over them without realizing it.

These verses make the same point as the preceding two. The Pharisees spend too much time on cultivating the appearance of righteousness while neglecting to make themselves truly righteous.

Because walking over a grave could make a person ritually unclean (Num. 6:6; 19:16), people whitened the graves, with chalk or lime, so people would not accidentally walk on them.[29] It seems strange to refer to these tombs as "beautiful," but perhaps, as with other regulations and customs, people began to focus on the whitening process itself instead of the reason behind it.

What are the "bones" and "filth" inside the Pharisees? Matthew again refers to the Pharisees' hypocrisy. Worse than hypocrisy, however, their righteous exteriors cover their *"lawlessness."*

Can you imagine how the Pharisees must have responded to such an accusation? They had dedicated their lives to upholding the laws of God. Now they were being accused of having no regard for the Law at all!

Notice that Luke does not mention anything about whitewashing. Indeed, Luke has a somewhat more sinister view. He implies that people who come into contact with the Pharisees become unwittingly defiled, because they do not know about the corruption within.

Seventh Woe: Pharisees and Their Prophets

Matthew 23:[29]Woe to you, scribes and Pharisees, hypocrites! For you build the tombs of the prophets and decorate the graves of the righteous, [30]and you say, "If we had lived in the days of our ancestors, we would not have taken part with them in shedding the blood of the prophets." [31]Thus you testify against yourselves that you are descendants of those who murdered the prophets. [32]Fill up, then, the

Luke 11:[47]Woe to you! For you build the tombs of the prophets whom your ancestors killed.

[48]So you are witnesses and ap-

measure of your ancestors. [33]You snakes, you brood of vipers! How can you escape being sentenced to hell? [34]Therefore I send you prophets, sages, and scribes, some of whom you will kill and crucify, and some you will flog in your synagogues and pursue from town to town, [35]so that upon you may come all the righteous blood shed on earth, from the blood of righteous Abel to the blood of Zechariah son of Barachiah, whom you murdered between the sanctuary and the altar. [36]Truly I tell you, all this will come upon this generation.

prove of the deeds of your ancestors; for they killed them, and you build their tombs. [49]Therefore also the Wisdom of God said, "I will send them prophets and apostles, some of whom they will kill and persecute," [50]so that this generation may be charged with the blood of all the prophets shed since the foundation of the world, [51]from the blood of Abel to the blood of Zechariah, who perished between the altar and sanctuary. Yes, I tell you, it will be charged against this generation.

No doubt the Pharisees, as people of the Book, had felt horror when they read of how the Judeans treated the prophet Jeremiah as he warned them of their impending defeat at the hands of the Babylonians (Jer. 38). They knew that they would never have sent Micaiah ben Imlah to prison for telling the truth (1 Kings 22). No doubt the Pharisees believed they had learned from their history. They would not fall into the same patterns of injustice and idol worship that their ancestors had. When Jesus makes a "like father, like son" observation about the current generation, his listeners probably felt appalled.

Put yourself in the place of people, who, mindful of their tragic history, had sworn their lives never to stray from the Law again as their ancestors had. Now imagine Jesus telling you that your dedication to that Law makes you just as bad as your ancestors.

For the members of the early Christian church, who had seen religious leaders persecute and perhaps kill some of their number, these words would have hit home. Prophets *had* arisen, the foremost one being Jesus Christ. And look what had happened to him. Although crucifixion was a Roman form of death penalty, not Jewish, the first Christians, steeped in the hostility between the church and synagogue and their own feelings of rejection, wanted the Jews blamed for Jesus' death. The reference to getting flogged in the synagogues may have reflected what was happening at the time the Gospel of Matthew achieved written form.

The term *brood of vipers* has parallels in both Matthew 3:7 and Luke 3:7, although it is John the Baptist who uses the phrase. In Luke 3:7, he condemns all those who listen to him, comparing them to snakes fleeing from a field that is being harvested or burnt.[30]

Abel is the first person murdered, according to the Hebrew Bible (Gen. 4:8; Heb. 11:4). The last recorded is in 2 Chronicles 24:18-22. After *Zechariah* son of Jehoiada denounced idol worship of the Judeans, King Joash had him stoned to death "in the court of the house of the Lord." Zechariah son of Berechiah is the prophet responsible for the book of Zechariah, but there is no record of him having been murdered. The sense of Matthew 23:35 is that since creation, a lot of righteous people have died at the hands of the unrighteous, and the people listening to Jesus will have to pay for it.

Think again of the early Christian community, whose Master had recently been crucified. Grief and bitterness have likely shaped the memory of Jesus' confrontation with the Pharisees. And yet, as noted above (chapter 3), the Romans and the chief priests had more to do with condemning Jesus to death than did the Pharisees. Jesus himself was reaching out to relate to the Pharisees. This showed that he accepted them as persons, appealed to them, and did not ignore them.

• • •

The anger of Matthew 23:1-36 can leave the reader a bit breathless. For those who have read little else about the Pharisees, this passage could lead them to believe the Pharisees practiced villainy of the first order. As this chapter has reiterated several times, we must read Matthew 23 in the context of the other Gospels and of the period when it achieved written form.

However, it might not hurt to examine why Matthew 23 makes us uncomfortable when it says such ugly things. The purpose of the Bible is not to make us comfortable. Ugly things happen in the Bible. We can find accounts of incest (Gen. 19:30-36), cannibalism (2 Kings 6:25-31) and adultery (2 Sam. 11:3-5) in it. And lest you believe that the Hebrew Bible is home to all uncomfortable passages in the Bible, remember that Jesus said many things we still find difficult to handle today. Why would he compare God to a corrupt judge (Luke 18:3-8)? Why would he compare a Gentile woman seeking his help to a dog (Mark 7:25-30)? Why would he tell his followers to sell their cloaks and buy swords (Luke 22:36)?

We should not fall into the habit of thinking that studying the Bible should make us comfortable. Instead, we should accept the fact that some of the reasons a text appears as it does are not obvious to the modern reader. We do not know precisely why Jesus said some of these things or how the tradition shaped his words to meet current needs. The hostility of Matthew 23 is not "wrong." It is hostility. Some people got hostile back then. Some people still do today.

For Discussion

1. How do you react to the parable of the prodigal son in Luke 15:11-32? Do you think the father was "fair" to the older brother? Why or why not?

Try to imagine a similar situation happening in your family.

2. What words would Jesus use today if he were criticizing you or your church for some of the same failings he saw in the Pharisees?

3. Would you rather have a church full of Pharisees or a church full of criminals? What would be a good ratio of each?

4. Can you think of some instances when people learned from past mistakes? Some times when they didn't?

5

How Jesus' Critique of the Pharisees Applies to Us

From the *Oxford English Dictionary:*

Pharisaic . . . 1. Of or belonging to the Pharisees

1643 Milton *Divorce* II.vi, He . . . removes the Pharisaick mists rais'd between the Law and the peoples eyes. **1678** Cudworth *Intell. Syst.* I.i.4.6, The Pharisaick Sect amongst the Jews. **1879** C. Geikie *Christ* 22, The bitterest persecutions of the Pharisaic party.

2. Resembling the Pharisees in being strict in doctrine and ritual, without the spirit of piety; laying great stress upon the external observances of religion and outward show of morality, and assuming superiority on that account; hypocritical; formal; self-righteous.

The particular connotation varies according as one or other of the aspects in which the Pharisees appear in the Gospels is emphasized; the present tendency being to emphasize that of self-righteousness.

1618 Sylvester *Alls not gold* xxiv, Wee are so Punctuall and Precise In Doctrine (Pharisaik-wise). **1771** Fletcher *Checks* Wks. 1795 II.13, He sets up pharisaic self, instead of Christ. **1795** Southey *Soldier's Funeral* 56, O my God! I thank thee, with no Pharisaic pride I thank thee, that I am not such as these. **1884** *Congregational Yr Bk.* 86, There is something worse than Pharisaic respectability. There is Pharisaic vice.

Pharisaical . . . = PHARISAIC

1538 Bale *Thre Lawes* 1604, As Cayphas ones sayd in counsell pharysaycall. **1613** Purchas *Pilgrimage* (1614) 124, The want of which office Christ objected to another of his Pharisaicall hostes. **1831** Burton *Eccl. Hist.* viii (1845) 189, The Pharisaical part of the Council declared him to be innocent. . . . **1531** Tindale *Exp. I John ii.3* (1537), Our Pharisaycall doctors haue no doctrine to knowe when a man is in the state of grace. **1625** Bacon *Ess., Superstition* (Arb.) 347, The causes of Superstition are: . . . Excesse of Outward and Pharisaicall Holinesse. **1794** G. Adams *Nat. & Exp. Philos.* II.xx.371, The Pharisaical self-sufficiency of the modern infidel. **1835** J. H. Newman *Par. Serm.* (1837) I.xi.161, There are vast multitudes of Pharisaical hypocrites among baptized Christians.

Hence **Pharisaically** *adv.*; **Pharisaicalness**

1599 *Broughton's Let.* vii.21, So farre houen with surquedrie and self-loue, . . . Pharisaically . . . to annihilate all others. **1679** Puller *Moder. Ch. Eng.* xvii.489, Their many kinds of Superstitions and Pharisacalness. **1884** *Bookseller* 6 Nov. 3177/2, He, pharisaically, in the interests of morality; gets the thief, whom he taught, committed to prison.

Pharisaism . . . 1. The doctrine and practice of the Pharisees; the fact of being a Pharisee. . . . **1882** Farrar *Early Chr.* I.519, It was the desire to preserve that Law intact which . . . formed the nobler side of Pharisaism.

2. The character and spirit of the Pharisees; hypocrisy; formalism; self-righteousness

1601 W. Watson *Import. Consid.* (1831) 27, You should not be seduced by Pharisaism, hypocrisy, and plausible persuasions. **1711** *Reflect. on Walls Hist. Inf. Bapt.* 351, What at length do you find, but a kind of men mad with Pharisaism, bewitching with traditions? **1874** Pusey *Lent. Serm.*

167, Of all the Pharisaisms of our day, our church going seems to me the masterpiece. **1879** Farrar *St. Paul* iii.I.46, When we speak of Pharisaism we mean obedience petrified into formalism, religion degraded into ritual, morals cankered by casuistry. . . .

Pharisee . . . 1. [An] ancient Jewish sect distinguished by their strict observance of the traditional and written law and by their pretensions to superior sanctity . . .

2. A person of Pharisaic spirit or disposition; a self-righteous person; a formalist; a hypocrite

1589 G. Harvey *Advt. Pappe Hatchet* Wks. (Grosart) II.193, Reprobates, . . . tyrants, pharises, hypocrites, false prophets. **1593** Nashe *Four Lett. Confut.* Wks. (Grosart) II.193, Though he play the Pharisie neuer so in justifying his owne innocence, theres none will beleeue him. . . . **1781** Cowper *Truth* 59, The peacock, see—mark what a sumptuous Pharisee is he! **1901** "Lucas Malet" *Sir R. Calmady* II.iii, I was a self-righteous little Pharisee—forgive me. . . .

Phariseeism . . . =PHARISAISM

1585 Fetherstone tr. *Calvin on Acts* xv.7.355, There remained no Phariseisme in Paul. **1865** L. Oliphant *Picadilly* vi. (1870) 221, The force and despotic power of the Phariseeism of the present day.[1]

In the last chapter, we examined two passages that contained a largely comprehensive summary of Jesus' criticisms of the Pharisees.

They are as follows:

1. The Pharisees were self-righteous.
2. The Pharisees were exclusive.
3. The Pharisees were show-offs and sought prestige.
4. The Pharisees were hypocrites.
5. The Pharisees were oppressive and hard-hearted.
6. The Pharisees were legalistic.
7. The Pharisees were nitpickers or had "tunnel vision."

8. The Pharisees persecuted the prophets and other righteous people.

In this chapter, we will examine the accusations lodged against the Pharisees and then look at the contemporary North American religious scene and see which of these accusations apply to it.

The comparisons will not always be exact. There are many ways in which the contemporary North American religious scene does not parallel the first-century Palestinian religious setting. We no longer have kings and emperors. Christianity has become a religion of the mainstream; people of other religions are now the odd ones out. While we do have social class distinctions, it is considered in bad taste to point them out.

Nevertheless, a good many of the charges lodged against the Pharisees do apply to us on different levels: personal, congregational, national, and global.

Self-Righteousness

In her autobiography, *Testament of Youth,* Vera Brittain describes her younger brother Edward: "At sixteen, he was inclined to be rather priggish and self-righteous—not such bad qualities in adolescence after all, since most of us have to be self-righteous before we can be righteous."[2]

As we grow older and accrue failures and losses, we learn to come to terms with our inadequacies. As young people, we might believe that others have no excuse for seeking divorce or becoming poor. If they would just try harder, we reason, they wouldn't let such things happen to them. As we grow older and such things do happen to us, we revise our thinking and view our youthful self-righteousness with tolerant chagrin.

Unfortunately, of course, some people never outgrow their self-righteousness. Like the Pharisee in Luke 18, they observe sharply the differences between their "good" behavior and the sinful behavior of others.

We have all known self-righteous people in the course of our church affiliations. We can think of the prim men and women who do not drink, smoke, dance, etc., and show little Christian love for those who do. Yet even we "right-thinking" people need to take a look at some of the ways we judge others.

We may decry racism and war and through our money and time, support institutions which fight these evils. From this position, we easily move to sneering at bigots and refusing to associate with those affiliated with the military. It is hard to admit that we are self-righteous when we do so.

During my first year in college, friends introduced me to the book, *Living More with Less,*[3] which called Christians to live a more "compassionate" (as opposed to simple) lifestyle. Soon I used scrap paper for all my writing, including letters and class papers. I took pride—and I do mean pride—in the fact that all my clothes came from thrift shops (except, of course, for the clothes that my parents had been so insensitive as to purchase new for me).

My sister was in junior high at the time and had developed a passion, along with the rest of her friends, for fashionable clothes. When I was home on breaks, I lectured her (there is no better word for it) about her materialism, trying to make her understand how she promoted poverty throughout the world.

As one might expect, the only change in behavior these lectures provoked was a sharper antagonism between myself and my sister. Years later, she and her husband now make conscious lifestyle decisions, based partly on the neediness of their fellow human beings. I've never asked, but I am sure my self-righteous preaching had nothing to do with this change.

What is the moral of this story? I had made my adherence to the principles of *Living More with Less* into an idolatry. Changing my lifestyle down to the smallest particulars became more important to me than building a good relationship with my sister. I used the positive, life-affirming principles to make myself "simpler-than-thou," and in the process I had shut out other people. I felt disdain for people who dressed fashionably and used plain white envelopes (instead of using old ones, or folding their letters so they didn't need envelopes). I looked with scorn upon people who ate fast food.

As soon as people make a commitment to living "righteous" lives, self-righteousness seems to come in and ruin it. We look at other people who do not have our self-discipline and judge them accordingly. Hence, we see people with AIDS, lung cancer, and cirrhosis of the liver and may feel compassion for them. Yet that ugly little glop of pride in us reminds us that we do not have these diseases because we do not use IV drugs, engage in promiscuous sex, smoke, or drink.

To counteract this self-righteousness, some people might point out that even people who live healthy lifestyles succumb to cancer, heart disease, etc. People have received AIDS from blood transfusions, accidents in medical care, and unfaithful spouses.

I believe Christ would have taken a more radical position, however. The point of Luke 18:9-14 for us is that any given upright Christian, no matter how loving, kind, and faithful, is no more righteous than any promiscuous drug dealer. They just happen to sin in different areas of their life. (If upright Christians sin in no other way, they almost certainly fall into the sin of self-righteousness.) Both types of people have the same need to confess their sins and ask forgiveness.

When Jesus said that the Sabbath was made for the

benefit of people rather than the other way around (Mark 2:27), he stated a principle that applies to all of the laws and commandments in the Bible. God gave us these laws because he *loves* us. Following these laws makes it easier for us to become complete human beings. Abusing our bodies or alienating other people in the end will always lead to unhappiness, which God does not want for us.

However, we make a mistake when we assume that following these laws wins us brownie points with God. It is as though someone hobbling around on crutches thinks he or she is superior to those people who do not have crutches. The crutches were made to help that person get around. They were not intended to be status symbols. It might sadden God to see that some people choose not to use the crutches he would provide. He might ache for the people who sit unhappily in passive immobility. But God does not consider these people of less worth than those who have sensibly decided to use the crutches provided.

When we move beyond the personal level, we can see that self-righteousness occurs on corporate levels as well. European and North American churches are still reacting to the patronizing philosophies of mission that were standard for most of the past centuries. We no longer speak of the white man's burden to manage and convert the heathen. Yet it is hard for many church members to reach out to those less fortunate without some degree of satisfaction that they are not in the same place. Instead of feeling gratitude and amazement that we have enough to eat, places to live, and a loving Christian community to support us, we begin to see these gifts from God as signs that we are God's favorites.

On a national and global level as well, a similar self-righteousness prevails. Those nations that have superior monetary or military power assume that all aspects of their culture must be superior to that found in the rest of the world. We refer to the "primitive" art of less-developed countries and become disgusted with their more flexible attitudes toward time commitments.

Self-righteousness, by definition, condemns all who exemplify it, because no one is righteous but God alone (Luke 18:19).

Exclusivity

In chapter 3 we learned that inclusivity is a major theme in the Gospel of Luke. Many of Jesus' teachings in Luke focus on the breaking down of barriers that kept people out of the kingdom of God. Jesus opened the gates to Samaritans, Gentiles, tax collectors, and all repentant sinners.

Today, most Christians at least pay lip service to the idea that the church should not shut out people because of their race or social status. Yet we all have different ways of excluding people.

Most of us feel more comfortable around people who are like ourselves. Even when we consider ourselves broad-minded and interested in other cultures, we nevertheless avoid certain people. Often we find ourselves tongue-tied around people with mental or physical disabilities. Most of us do not make a point of establishing relationships with prostitutes as Jesus did. We would just as soon that criminals remain in prison and out of our sight.

For centuries, raging debates have arisen over whom the church should include or exclude. Today in many denominations, people argue about who should be admitted to communion. As I write this, one of the conferences in my denomination is trying to decide whether to kick out a congregation that admits homosexuals into its membership.

Questions of inclusivity and exclusivity have special relevance for denominations with a strong tradition of church discipline. These churches take seriously the words of Matthew 18:15-20 and in practice have excluded erring members of their churches.

The Mennonite and Amish churches have called this tradition "banning." Members of the church are to shun and not have social and business dealings with the banned person. Few of the mainstream Mennonite churches practice shunning anymore. A lot of people who remember church discipline from their childhood shudder when they recount the times that pregnant teenage girls had to stand up in front of their congregations to confess their sins or else suffer excommunication.

On the other hand, I knew someone in college who told me that one of the elders in his Mennonite church worked in a nuclear weapons facility. No one had confronted this man over the evident contradiction in his choosing to remain a member of a committed peace church while helping to construct weapons of mass destruction. My friend wondered whether shunning had been such a bad idea after all.

What do we do when part of the gospel tells us to welcome sinners and parts of it tells us to cast them from our midst? We can say that church should be open to all who repent, but that does not present a perfect answer to the question. What about people who drink and dance? These activities are not absolutely forbidden in the Bible, but neither are they condoned by many of our churches today. Should historic peace churches welcome members of the military into their midst? What about wealthy corporate executives?

These unanswered and maybe unanswerable questions overshadow all the ways in which our churches exclude people unintentionally. We exclude when we do not build our churches to make them accessible to people with disabilities, when we emphasize family events that might exclude singles, when we turn away strangers who ask for our help.

On a national level, we practice exclusivity in our immigration laws. As I write these words, the United States has denied entrance to thousands of Haitians in spite of the documented human-rights abuses in that country following the ouster of Jean Bertrand Aristide. At the same time the U.S. Immigration and Naturalization Service welcomes any Cuban immigrant asking for asylum. On a global level, rich nations practice exclusion of the poor. In the United Nations, first attention is given to the economic powers of the world. We hear and learn about affluent cultures, while those living in absolute poverty around the world live and die in anonymity.

Showing Off

One of the older women in my church told me that in the church community where she grew up, people considered pride an overwhelming concern. If someone complimented a woman on her pies, she would insist that all merit accrue to the person who had given her the recipe in the first place. If someone would congratulate a farmer on a prize pig, he would attribute the pig's fine qualities to the stock it came from rather than to his animal husbandry skills. Unfortunately, as the woman recalled, this fear of pride often affected children in damaging ways. If a child had done particularly well at school or drawn an outstanding picture, the parent would insist that these achievements had nothing to do with offspring's skill and would find some excuse to show that the child only appeared to have achieved something superior, but in reality had no more talent than any other child.

At the opposite extreme, I remember an evangelist who came to speak on a Christian emphasis day at my college. For nearly an hour he boasted of having personally brought over a thousand people to Christ. At the time, I gave a lot of credit to my fellow students when not one of them came forward as the wheezy organ started playing "Just as I Am."

The Catholic Church tradition regards pride as the worst of the seven deadly sins, with good reason. Human pride lies at the root of almost all the atrocities committed in the name of religion throughout history. We will examine some of these atrocities in chapter 6.

We can point to people who manifest obvious aspects of pride. But even Christians who conscientiously avoid the appearance of pride and want to be humble, can find themselves stumbling into hidden pitfalls of vanity.

As I mentioned in the section on self-righteousness, adherents of simple living can easily fall into the trap of thinking themselves superior to those who dress fashionably, wear makeup, do not recycle, and so on. For some people, dressing in ragged clothing represents as much pride on their part as the wearing of large phylacteries or ostentatious prayer shawls did on the part of certain Pharisees. People who commit themselves to voluntary service and missions may subconsciously seek exactly the same prestige as those Pharisees who occupied Moses' seat in the synagogue.

Whole churches can manifest the sin of pride. We might conveniently think of Jim and Tammy Bakker and Heritage USA. The Bakkers promoted themselves and the Heritage "evangelical" theme park as unabashedly as any used-car salesman. When the public learned of Jim Bakker's sexual misconduct and the massive fraud he had perpetrated during his fundraising, many Christians felt an inward satisfaction that Proverbs 16:18 had proved true: "Pride goes before destruction, and a haughty spirit before a fall." And those who felt such satisfaction themselves committed the sins of pride and self-righteousness.

All nationalism is a form of pride. Christians are right to feel wary when their country begins to flaunt itself as the bastion of every virtue. Normally, this happens when the government has chosen to do something particularly despicable, such as invading a less-powerful country. Many Christians in the United States shuddered when they witnessed the hoopla surrounding the invasions of Grenada and Panama. Soldiers returned from the 1991 Persian Gulf war to celebrations far exceeding those for veterans of the Korean and Vietnam wars, even though our army had devastated the Iraqi army within a few days.

However, it is too easy for us to point to nationalism and television evangelism as outstanding examples of human pride. Pride occurs in all levels of human society. To boast of becoming the first church to offer sanctuary to Salvadoran refugees demonstrates as much vanity as to boast of a million-dollar pipe organ the church has installed. To feel pride at deliberately living below the poverty level so that taxes will not go to support the military is as reprehensible as feeling proud of owning a BMW.

If every good thing we do can become a source of pride, how then can we function as the human beings God means us to be? The obvious answer is that we can't, because we are human beings. To get beyond this pessimistic observation, however, we might look at the things we do each day for which we do not receive any special acclaim. When we change a dirty diaper, we do not save it and say, "Look at this diaper I changed!" We change the diaper because it needs to be done. We have an obligation to care for our children.

In the same way, we must do justice and practice peace out of thankfulness to God and joyful response for the overwhelming grace we have received. This is our obligation to God. We do nothing "special" when we practice justice—even if it is rare in our society. We merely do our duty. If we could only not feel so proud of having done our duty!

Hypocrisy

In Matthew 23, hypocrisy seems to be the thread which binds together all of Jesus's accusations against the Pharisees. At the very beginning of the diatribe, he says, "The scribes and the Pharisees sit on Moses' seat; therefore, do whatever they teach you and follow it; but do not do as they do, for they do not practice what they teach." He then accuses them of hypocrisy seven more times throughout the rest of the chapter.

Few people tolerate the vice of hypocrisy, except in politics. The public seems ruefully to accept the need to refer to bombing raids as "pacification of enemy forces." When President Reagan championed the rights of the unborn in the 1980s while at the same time supporting the antigovernment forces in Nicaragua who bombed day-care centers and hospitals, few thought to point out the hypocrisy of these positions.

Away from the political realm, however, no one likes a hypocrite. Church people, in particular, come under the scrutiny of the unchurched for signs of hypocrisy. Woe to the Christian businessperson who grows rich while employees of that business struggle to subsist on meager wages. Woe to the sharp-tongued elder who gossips and criticizes the lives of all who come into contact with him or her.

We can all think of stereotypes of hypocritical Christians who seem to hold others to a higher standard than they hold themselves. However, when we ask ourselves how we behave as hypocrites, it becomes harder. Those blessed with teenage children will have the good fortune to have their hypocrisy pointed out to them. Indeed, parents often have to squirm as they think of times they have demanded that their children behave in a certain way when they themselves had fallen short in the same area. Many parents who smoke or engage in other self-destructive behaviors forbid their children to do likewise. On a smaller, less-obvious scale, we may rebuke our children for speaking unkindly to one of their playmates. Yet we ourselves do not speak to our own children with the same respect that we may use when speaking to another child.

The one good thing we can say about hypocrites is that they at least perceive what is the right thing to do, even if they do not live up to their perception. In a sense all Christians live hypocritical lives. Like the Pharisees, we have a good idea of what God expects of us, but we do not follow through on this knowledge.

Hard-Heartedness

In Matthew 23:4, Jesus says that the Pharisees "tie up heavy burdens, hard to bear, and lay them on the shoulders of others; but they themselves are unwilling to lift a finger to move them." As mentioned in chapter 4, one can interpret this verse in a couple different ways. According to the most obvious interpretation, the Pharisees saddled believers with many extra regulations and then did nothing to help and support these believers as they sought to live a life faithful to God.

In chapter 4, we mentioned the "fence around the Torah" built of oral Torah, later written in the Mishnah. Again, the purpose of the oral Torah was to help people keep the law, not to trip them up. All the rules and regulations governing the Sabbath were meant to serve as a safety net that would help the devout Jew to keep the Sabbath holy.[4] When taken in the right spirit, these regulations were (and still are) a blessing to those who followed them.

Every denomination builds its own "fences" around

biblical commandments in order to aid their followers to live more faithfully. In the Catholic Church the rites of the Eucharist developed from a sincere desire to follow Christ's instructions given during the Last Supper.

Other churches have sought to keep their members safe from sexual transgressions by forbidding dancing or the consumption of alcohol. In Bible times, dancing seemed customary during celebrations.[5] The consumption of wine was also taken for granted (remember Jesus' first sign in John 2:1-11).

However, alcohol serves to lessen inhibitions, as anyone who has experienced the buzz of a first drink will tell you. Dancing can help spark an erotic charge between persons not committed to each other. Since drinking and dancing can easily lead people into sexual temptation, some churches have sought safety in their prohibition.

Again, human nature has a way of twisting the goodness out of any rule. The Catholic rite of the Eucharist, a holy and mysterious celebration of faith and community, has been twisted by certain people throughout the centuries into an act of superstitious magic. Those who grew up in houses that forbade alcohol may remember the fascinated revulsion they felt when they first saw a bottle of wine and the harsh judgments they made of the people who drank from it.

When we begin to use rules to exclude and condemn others, when failure to meet one of many regulations makes us feel we have failed God, then those rules have ceased to act as a fence around (or a safety net under) Scripture. When rules like these become oppressive and make us harden our hearts toward those who violate them, we need to hop over the fence and take a good look at what the Bible really says.

Legalism

I went to the Mennonite World Conference in Winnipeg in 1990. The first night my mother and I were there, we went to worship in the Winnipeg hockey arena. Hearing 17,000 Christians singing in four-part harmony in many different languages made my emotions soar almost uncontrollably. In the midst of my spiritual reverie, the right arm of the man in front of me shot up in a gesture of praise.

"Oh," I thought. "*Now* I understand."

I had friends and family who belonged to churches involved with the charismatic movement. While I tried to respect their worship practices, I did not really understand why they worshiped the way they did. A worship service at an affluent charismatic church in my hometown left me cold. If I were honest, I would admit that I might have felt more comfortable attending a service in some African country. I could have appreciated the dancing and arm-waving in an African church. In the United States, they seemed, well, foreign.

But when that man's arm went up in the hockey arena at Winnipeg, my heart shot up with it. I understood what it meant to feel so full of a spirit of joy that part of one's body just had to show it. I think I cried.

Then as the week progressed, during morning and evening worship, I noticed that some people put their hands up mechanically every time certain catch phrases appeared in hymns or in the addresses of the speakers. I am sure that the cold rationality I brought into my observations affected my perceptions. Yet I know that most of those people could not have felt the soaring joy of that first night every single time they raised their arms. I had no objection to it as a mode of worship, any more than I object to Catholics genuflecting, Protestants standing during hymns, or Jews swaying during prayer. It just made me reflect that all human attempts to interact with the Holy have a tendency to degenerate into formulas.

Like self-righteousness, pride, and hypocrisy, legalism seems to be a part of the human condition. Every spiritual expression can and will become legalistic. The Catholic religious orders and the Amish, as part of their desire to live simple and holy lifestyles, initially wore the clothing of simple working folk. As times passed and styles changed, they continued to wear these clothes to demonstrate that they did not follow the worldly dictates of fashion. Today, the Amish, Old Order Mennonites, and certain orders of monks and nuns continue to wear clothes that reflect the styles of the eighteenth century and earlier. The original purpose of plain clothes and habits—to dress like the poor—has been replaced by a desire to wear clothing that signals identity and community.

Some churches, in order not to get tied up in the letter of the law, consciously use innovative worship forms and informal attire. One Sunday when attending a charismatic church, I was amused to read in the bulletin that the official guidelines of this particular charismatic movement encouraged informal attire. Sure enough, the people attending conscientiously wore sporty clothes from the better catalogs. Informal attire and overhead projectors can become just as formulaic as robes and hymnals.

Many people try for self-discipline in their spiritual lives by planning daily devotional times and Bible reading. These devotional times should bring believers closer to God, but too soon daily reading, done with the regularity of brushing one's teeth, can take on the spiritual significance of brushing one's teeth. We rush through another psalm in time to go to work.

This does not mean that we should only pray or study God's Word when we feel like it. Doing so when we do not feel like it builds spiritual discipline. Likewise, we should tithe whether we want to or not. The letter of the law has some value if it helps us fulfill our religious obligations in spite of our desires. Unfortunately, our human nature will inevitably turn the spiritual into the legal in order to make it easier for us to grasp.

Gnat-picking

In 1989-90, the National Endowment for the Arts came under attack in the United States because of provocative artwork done under its auspices by Andres Serrano and Robert Mapplethorpe. Much of Mapplethorpe's photography was frankly pornographic, and Serrano's infamous photo showed a plastic crucifix in a container of urine.

Senator Jesse Helms, outraged by these photographs, spearheaded a drive to eliminate funding for the National Endowment of the Arts. After a time, in reaction to his obsession with these distasteful and/or blasphemous artistic renditions, people began to question Helms's emphasis. With North Carolina having the second highest infant mortality rate in the country,[6] people asked why his attention was so focused on obscene art. Helms vigorously supports the tobacco industry in his state. Given how many deaths result from consumption of tobacco each year, people asked why he picked an assault on the NEA to safeguard society.

On October 19, 1992, the Louisiana State Supreme Court ruled that prisoners could not be forced to take medication against their will. This decision reversed one made in 1989, when the court said Michael O. Perry, a death-row inmate, could be forced to take antipsychotic medicine. He is insane when not on that medicine, and his family and lawyers fought to keep him *off* antipsychotics. The laws of Louisiana say that the state cannot execute criminals who are mentally ill. Therefore, the state of Louisiana wanted to forcibly inject him with antipsychotic medicine *so it could execute* this prisoner.

Perry, no longer competent to make these sorts of choices, lives in a hallucinatory hell so that he may remain alive.[7] In order to remain faithful to the letter of the law, the Louisiana courts overlooked the more important question of whether the death penalty is just at all.

Sometimes gnats seem bigger and more important than camels. The tendency to develop a tunnel vision, focusing on minute details, relates to the tendency in human nature to change the spiritual into the legal. Legalism entails following a formula, and formula consists of smaller component parts. Thus in our desire to do the right thing, we try to attend to details and miss the bigger picture.

Government bureaucracies often show an obsession with detail. The state of New York has a somewhat more progressive approach to care of the developmentally disabled than many states in the U.S. It was one of the first states to move people out of institutions and into group homes. Yet these group homes themselves became subject to a bewildering variety of state regulations—many of which seem picayune, such as the precise number of inches from the ceiling and the floor that food must be stored.

Many workers in the human services view New York State's Active Treatment Programming as the worst sort of nit-picking. Active Treatment applies to group homes that house residents with disabilities such as profound mental retardation, severe physical disabilities, or extreme behavioral problems. It specifies that no resident may go for longer than five minutes without engaging in a goal specified in the person's Active Treatment Program.

I used to work at an agency that provided homes for developmentally disabled adults. As part of my work, I attended a seminar at which one of the inspectors for New York State's Office of Mental Retardation and Developmental Disabilities spoke.

He said, "If I were to walk into one of your homes and see one of the staff interacting in a positive manner with one of the residents—I mean, they're just spending time with each other and enjoying each other's company—I would cite you for violating state regulations, unless you could tell me how this interaction fit into that resident's Active Treatment Program. The taxpayers aren't paying you to be friends with the residents."

Throughout the agency, all residents who lived in homes falling under the Active Treatment Programming regulations soon had "socialization goals."

In my work in the Supportive Apartments which the agency ran, I spent hours every day making phone calls, filling out paperwork, and attending meetings to discuss what would facilitate each adult's ability to live independently. At the end of a shift, when it was time for me to visit some of the adults in their apartment to help them cook supper or work on a money goal, I found myself grudging the time because of all the paperwork I needed to get done. At such times, I had to give myself a mental kick and remind myself that I had taken this job because I wanted to serve people. Although the paperwork needed to get done, it was far less important, in the long run, than making human contact. The paperwork and meetings diverted my attention, like annoying little gnats, from the camel of human neglect that lay before me.

In our churches, gnats can catch our attention in a variety of ways. Oddly enough, people often have the ability to shoo them away when attending to larger issues. The decision for my home church to become a sanctuary for Central American refugees occasioned little debate. It was the question of carpeting the sanctuary that *really* divided the church. Each side had good reasons for carpeting or not carpeting. But in the heat of the discussion, larger issues such as building community and consensus temporarily got short shrift.

I attended a meeting of an ecumenical council in my community as an observer. Our Mennonite fellowship was considering whether to join. Representatives spent the first hour arguing about two words in the statement of purpose. They were controversial words—having to do with a bias against homosexuals—but the rancor of the debate convinced me that our fellowship did not want to be a part of this organization. Yet many of the same churches worked together in a true Christian spirit when Habitat for Humanity built several houses for low-income people in the city. In a sense, perhaps we should feel appreciation for the times when larger Christian issues seem easy. If only the small issues could be decided as easily.

Persecuting Prophets

One of the most stunning accusations Jesus makes against the Pharisees is that they persecuted the prophets. The Pharisees were descended from people who, after returning from the exile, vowed never to become the unjust, corrupt society that had existed before Jerusalem fell. *This* time, they would heed what the prophets said. They would show their faithfulness to God in every aspect of life. They took seriously the words of prophets who stated that God wanted his people to live holy lives more than he wanted their sacrifices (as in Isa. 1:11-17).

When society's morals change, it is easy to look back at the times before these changes and say, "If I would have lived back then, I would not have owned slaves," or "I would have hidden Jews from the Nazis, too." We cannot, in fairness, make these assumptions in our own era.

Unless we had lived in the South and had loved and respected friends and family members who owned slaves, we cannot really imagine the courage it would have taken to tell these people that owning other human beings was evil. Unless we lived in Nazi-occupied Europe and knew that the Nazis would hang our own children from balconies (as was the case in Poland) if they found us hiding Jews, we cannot assume we would have easily agreed to hide anyone fleeing from Nazi persecution. In short, we can never count the cost of faithfulness in any era but our own.

So who are the prophets today? The original sense of the word *prophet* is "one who speaks for God." We could probably add that prophets look beyond the cultural values of their time and speak the truth. We can look at national and global situations and pick out people who speak against war and injustice. Contrary to biblical tradition, a few have even received honor in their lifetimes. I think especially of Mother Teresa of Calcutta, who, oddly enough in this world, became famous for her goodness and has used that fame to fight poverty.

Most prophets are not so fortunate. Admittedly, most of them are not as likable as Mother Teresa. Biblical tradition has it that many prophets acted rather strangely. Isaiah walked around naked for three years to warn the Judeans not to look to Egypt for help (Is. 20:2-4). He also named his sons "The-Spoil-Speeds-the-Prey-Hastens," and "A-Remnant-Will-Return" (Isa. 8:1-4; 7:3-4). Don't tell me they didn't get teased on the playground! Think of Jeremiah, who shouldered a yoke to dramatize God's unpopular assertion that the Judeans should submit to the Babylonians (Jer. 27:2.) Think of John the Baptist, roaming around the desert, wearing clothing made from camel's hair (itchy, especially in hot weather) and eating insects and honey (Mark 1:6).

Who are the people today who seem ridiculous to us, who yet feel an urgent need to speak the truth? How do we feel about street-corner preachers proclaiming the end times? How do we feel about environmentalists chaining themselves to trees? How do we feel about the people constantly getting arrested and re-arrested at nuclear weapons facilities? Looking at our own congregations, how do we feel about that old man who *always* stands up in the congregational meeting, just after everyone thinks the participants have achieved consensus, and says he feels compelled to represent the opposite view, "just so we look at all sides"?

Not everyone who preaches and demonstrates does so prophetically. Not everyone who presents a view contrary to public opinion speaks the truth. We need to keep in mind, however, that prophets tend to go against the norm in any society.

The story of Micaiah son of Imlah in 1 Kings 22 illustrates this point. The king of Israel and the King of Judah are debating whether to go to war with the king of Syria and recapture Ramoth-gilead. King Jehoshaphat of Judah is cautious and says he would feel more comfortable if they consulted God first. The king of Israel asks his four hundred prophets about going to battle with Syria (Aram), and they tell him his victory is a sure thing. King Jehoshaphat, evidently not as eager to go to war as the king of Israel, asks if there isn't another prophet they might consult.

> The king of Israel said to Jehoshaphat, "There is still one other by whom we may inquire of the Lord, Micaiah son of Imlah; but I hate him, for he never prophesies anything favorable about me, but only disaster." (1 Kings 22:8)

Naturally, Jehoshaphat really wants to hear Micaiah after having this piece of information. A servant, sent to fetch the prophet, warns him to speak favorably about the war as the other four hundred prophets have done. Micaiah replies, "As the Lord lives, whatever the Lord says to me, that I will speak." He tells the kings that he has seen a vision of sheep without a shepherd. Furthermore, he says that God wishes to "entice" Ahab (the king of Israel) to go up against the Syrians and so had put a "lying spirit" in the mouths of the four hundred prophets. The king of Israel has Micaiah thrown in jail and orders him fed on reduced rations of bread and water until he returns from Ramoth-gilead.

You may have guessed that the story does not end happily for the king of Israel. The Syrians kill him in battle. We don't know how it ended for Micaiah son of Imlah. Since the king never returned, one wonders if he was never released and lived on bread and water the rest of his days.

Like Micaiah son of Imlah, modern prophets may tell us things we do not like to hear. They may criticize our lifestyles and tell us that if we persist in a certain behavior, things will turn out badly for us. They may call to our attention the hypocrisy and self-righteousness in our Christian journey. They may point out our hard-heartedness toward those less fortunate, or perhaps toward those who just drive us up a wall.

When people tell us things we do not like to hear, we need to pause before we dismiss them, or before we set them up as our enemy. They may be ill-tempered and critical. They could be prophets. Or they could be both.

Conclusion

Over the years, I have come to the conclusion that the best things in life are the most easily perverted. Food can represent the coming together in table fellowship of the Christian community or it can become the obsession of the gluttonous, anorexic, or bulimic. Sex can build intimacy, love, and commitment in a marriage, or it can exploit the weak. Religion itself can represent humankind's closest encounter with God, or it can be a force which bullies and manipulates people.

We should keep this in mind when we examine our behavior and that of the Pharisees in the light of Scripture. Each of the negative traits examined in this chapter represents a digression from a pure and noble trait. Before self-righteousness, there is true righteousness. Before there is exclusivity, there is a desire for purity. Showing off one's virtue, indicates an appreciation for virtue. Hypocrisy implies a recognition of the right thing to do. In strictness, legalism, and nit-picking, we can find an earnest desire to live faithful lives, down to the smallest detail. Even in the persecution of the prophets, one might find the desire to preserve a tradition of faithfulness to God.

We have all sinned and fallen short of the glory of God, and we have all earnestly desired to overcome these sins. We have all been partly successful, and God has loved us even when we weren't.

For Discussion

1. I have written this chapter to show that most human beings, Christian and otherwise, possess the same weaknesses for which Jesus criticized the Pharisees.

Someone may ask, "So what if we *are* all Pharisees?" How would our churches and missions programs operate if every member tithed as rigorously as the Pharisees did? How would our home lives be different if we viewed every action as an act of worship to God? How would our lifestyles change if we viewed the Sabbath reverently?

2. Think of some times you have acted or spoken hypocritically. Now think of some times you have witnessed others acting or speaking hypocritically. In which case did you find it easiest to think of examples?

3. What are some of the activities you engage in so that you might live a more spiritual life? At what point do these activities become formula, and when do they help you to transcend formula? Think of a variety of world religions and denominations. In what ways do these religions promote spirituality? In what ways do these religions become legalistic?

4. What are some of the details you must attend to on an everyday basis? What are larger issues from which these details sometimes distract you? What are some of the small issues with which your church has dealt? What are large issues you have faced together? With which did the church deal most easily?

6

Christendom's Persecution of the Jews

The Prodigal Son: Part 3

The enmity between the older and younger brothers was passed down by each clan from generation to generation. Children and grandchildren did not quite understand why they hated each other, but they found it easy to hate, anyway.

It happened that the king of that land befriended a great-grandson of the younger brother, who had done him some service, and the king made a decree: from that time forward, his subjects should show special favor to the clan of the younger brother.

Those belonging to the clan of the older brother now found themselves regarded as outcasts. They faced hostility from the clan of the younger brother, and the inhabitants of the rest of the kingdom began to persecute them as well.

Centuries passed. Members of the clan of the older brother moved from country to country, nation state to nation state—anywhere they could live in peace and maintain their identity. They clung to certain traditions of the Father—that venerable ancestor to whom the older brother had remained loyal, while the shiftless younger brother had run off and wasted his inheritance. Because they maintained these traditions, many people in many countries found them odd. Some even felt a little afraid of them, because they seemed so different.

The king who had favored the clan of the younger brother became powerful, conquering many countries throughout the world. The people in these countries were told the ancient story of the two brothers, but the clan of the younger brother taught them a different ending. They told the people in every land that, when the younger brother returned, the Father had rejected the older brother and driven him from the house. For this reason, the clan of the older brother hated the clan of the younger brother and had persecuted it without mercy. They told many stories of horrible things the clan of the older had done to the clan of the younger. They accused the clan of the older of blasphemy, greed, murder, and cannibalism.

As the stories grew worse and worse with the passage of time, so did the treatment of the clan of the older. Members of the clan could no longer remember when they had lived in peace. They began to expect hatred and persecution, although they tried their best to keep away from the people they offended by their continuing existence.

People continued to take offense, however. War came to the world, and evil leaders united people through hatred of all who were different. They exterminated descendants of the older brother, save for a few who managed to escape. The clan of the younger brother and the rest of the world rejoiced that at long last the enmity that had lasted a thousand generations was over.

And when the Father returned to gather the remnant

who had survived the extermination, he dressed them in white robes and dried their tears. He bore them away to the country of all who had remained faithful. When they left, they took the light they had nurtured for centuries with them, and the world perished in darkness.

• • •

Two out of every five Jews living in the twentieth century have been murdered.[1]

In my Old Testament foundations class of my first seminary year, one of the students made a comment: "I don't understand why the Jews keep trying to give us a guilt complex by throwing the Holocaust in our faces." My professor was quiet for a moment and then remarked, "After what Christians have done to them for the last thousand years, I'm surprised that the Jews even speak to us."

The horror of the Holocaust still overwhelms us. Eleven million people dead in concentration camps. Six million Jewish men, women, and children murdered in the camps and in front of firing squads. Many died in even less humane ways. We may feel contempt for the right-wing neo-Nazi groups who claim that the Holocaust never happened. Yet we can in a small way understand why some might find the horror unbelievable. How could humanity have resorted to cruelty far beyond basic animal instincts?

To answer this question, we need to realize that it took centuries of hate to culminate in the Holocaust. Centuries of the church referring to the Jews as Christ-killers, centuries of rumor and innuendo about Jewish ritual murder, centuries of treating Jews like animals.

Some scholars trace the roots of anti-Semitism back to pagan times. Since the Jews had special privileges under the Roman empire that other minorities did not, a certain amount of jealousy existed among pagan peoples who also lived under Roman domination. Jewish ethnic solidarity provoked suspicion. Their difference was seen in many ways, notably in keeping the Sabbath and in refusing to recognize pagan gods in civil ceremonies. And admittedly, the scorn with which some Jews viewed Gentiles did not endear them to their Gentile neighbors.[2]

With the growth of Christianity, however, the demonization and the dehumanization of the Jewish people became widespread and entrenched.

The New Testament records early examples of Jewish-Christian hostilities. We know that some Jews forced Jewish-Christians out of the synagogues.[3] The stoning of Stephen in the book of Acts tells us that the Jewish-Christian conflict became violent at times. In A.D. 117 under the Emperor Trajan, Jews participated in bringing the death of Simeon, bishop of Jerusalem. Bar Kokhba, the leader of the second Jewish revolt in A.D. 132-135, killed Christians who refused to deny Christ.[4]

Hatred did not always or usually lead to violence, however. According to the writings of influential church leaders in the first few centuries, Jewish writers put out a considerable amount of anti-Christian propaganda. Justin Martyr, Tertullian, Eusebius, Hippolytus, and Origen all complained about the way Jews insulted the person of Christ. Some demeaning references to Christians are still found in the Palestinian Talmud. Rabbi Tarfon (ca. 80-110) asked that he be cursed if he did not burn Christian Scriptures, regardless of the fact that they contained the sacred name of God, because he considered Christians worse than heathens. Rabbi Meir (c. 135-170) called the Gospels "a revelation of sin."[5]

Christian writers of the first four centuries of this era did not turn the other cheek. Consider Ambrose, Bishop of Milan (ca. 340-397) who preached that the Jewish synagogue was a "house of impiety, a receptacle of folly, which God himself has condemned." His congregations subsequently burned down a synagogue. After the Jews protested to the emperor, Ambrose asked the emperor to spare his people punishment, saying that since the synagogues contained nothing of value, "what do the Jews lose by fire?"[6]

For anti-Jewish polemic, however, St. John Chrysostom (ca. 349-407) wins the prize. He preached, "The synagogue is worse than a brothel. . . . It is the den of scoundrels and the repair of wild beasts, . . . the temple of demons devoted to idolatrous cults, . . . the refuge of brigands and debauchees, and the cavern of devils." Referring to Jews in general, he wrote, "Debauchery and drunkenness had brought them to the level of the lusty goat and the pig. They know only one thing, to satisfy their stomachs, to get drunk, to kill and beat each other up like stage villains and coachmen." After arriving in Constantinople in 398, he persuaded the emperor to repeal all privileges to the Jews. In his "Sixth Homily Against the Jews," he wrote that God had deprived the Jews of their inheritance, following with, "Why then did he rob you [the Jews]? Is it not obvious that it was because he hated you, and rejected you once and for all? [7]

We need not excuse the early Christians and Jews who wrote spiteful invective against each other. But we need to understand the historical environment that gave birth to this invective in order to understand the horrors that came later. We need to understand that in the first three centuries, Christians and Jews more or less stood on equal footing as minority groups within the empire. They competed with each other for converts and jostled with each other for the position of being God's "real" chosen people.

All of that changed in A.D. 313, when the Roman Emperor Constantine converted to Christianity because he believed Christ had helped him win several battles in the previous two years.[8] Christianity now had the help and support of the emperor. Judaism could no longer compete.

After the second Jewish revolt in 132-135, the Romans drove the Jews out of Palestine. They continued to wander throughout the Roman empire, settling in hospitable lands and continuing to protect their identity as people of the Book. Until the tenth century, we do not have much on record about Jewish-Christian relationships—beyond knowing that Christian writers continued to write scornfully of the unbelieving Jews, and that Jews continued to live as outcasts on the fringes of society in most European countries.

The advent of the Middle Ages began a bloody millennium for Jewish history. This following chronology gives a sense of the unrelenting and widespread persecution the Jews have faced for the last thousand years. For ease of citation, unless otherwise indicated, I have taken all examples from Malcolm Hay's seminal work on *Europe and the Jews*.

Chronology of Anti-Semitism

1096 The beginning of the First Crusade. About ten thousand Jews in Western Europe are slaughtered as the Crusaders march to the coast and on to Jerusalem. Once in Jerusalem, they spend a week slaughtering the inhabitants there, including as part of this massacre shutting Jews up inside their synagogue and setting it on fire.[9]

1146 A renegade Cistercian monk tells recruits for the Second Crusade in Germany that it is their duty first to kill the Jews in their own country. Massacres begin in Spires, Cologne, Mainz, and other German cities.[10]

1171 A Christian groom in Blois, France, reports that he has seen a Jew throw the body of a child into the Loire River. No evidence is produced to indicate that a crime has been committed: no one in the region has reported a missing child, and no body is ever produced. Thirty-four Jewish men and seventeen Jewish women are tortured and burned at the stake.[11]

1182 King Philip of France drives the Jews out of his country, confiscating all their property. When the economy slumps as a result, he invites them back in 1198, an act that meets with the disapproval of Pope Innocent III.[12]

1208 Pope Innocent III, in a letter to the Count of Nevers, writes, "The Jews, against whom the blood of Jesus Christ calls out, although they ought not to be killed, lest the Christian people forget the Divine Law, yet as wanderers ought they to remain upon the earth, until their countenance be filled with shame."[13]

1215 The Fourth Lateran Council advises rulers to address the problem of usury, directing them not "to be aroused against the Christians because of this, but to try rather to keep the Jews from this practice." In addition to this ruling, the council forbids Jews to walk in public on specified days, especially during the Easter season. They may not wear their best clothes on Sundays and are to be fired from all public offices. Any money they have earned in these jobs is to be turned over to Christians.[14] Additionally, Pope Innocent III declares they must wear a badge in public identifying themselves as Jews.[15]

1236 In Fulda, Germany, crusaders put to the sword thirty-six Jews of both sexes on the unsubstantiated charge of having killed five sons of a miller and using the blood in their religious rituals.[16]

1240 A "trial" is held for the Talmud in Paris, and it is judged a blasphemous and heretical work. Twenty-four cartloads of Talmudic literature are burned.[17]

1243 "Scores" of Jews are burned alive outside Berlin after being accused of stealing eucharistic bread for their rituals.[18]

1247 Pope Innocent IV writes to condemn a nobleman, Draconet de Montauban, for mistreating the Jews of Vienne (a province in France):

> The noble Draconet despoiled the Jews of all their goods and cast them into a fearful prison, and without admitting the legitimate protestation and defense of their innocence, he cut some of them in two, others he burnt at the stake, of others he castrated the men and tore the breasts off the women. He afflicted them with divers other kinds of tortures, until, as it is said, they confessed with their mouth what their conscience did not dictate.

The churchmen in the vicinity, although not assisting in the tortures, do confiscate the properties of the remaining Jews. The pope orders all property returned. The Archbishop of Vienne takes no action, saying the presence of Jews in Vienne constitutes a threat to Christian souls.[19]

1252 Matthew Paris writes in his *Chronicle*, The King [of England] extorts from the Jews whatever visible property those wretched people possess, not only, as it were, skinning them merely, but also plucking out their entrails.[20]

1253 The Jews are driven out of France again—this time by King Louis. Caursin and Italian moneylenders rush in to fill the void and charge much higher interest rates.[21]

1254 Matthew Paris in a continuing account of the English king's extortion of the Jews, writes, "The King vented his fury against the wretched rabble of the Jews to such a degree they hated their lives." When they ask permission to leave the country because they can not afford to pay what is demanded of them, the King replies, "Whither could you fly, wretched beings? The French King hates you and persecutes you and has condemned you to perpetual banishment." The king's demands are backed up by the English clergy.[22]

1266 The Council of Breslau decrees that Jews may not live among Christians because the Christians "might fall easy prey to the influence of the superstitious and evil habits of the Jews living among them." The Council of Vienna in 1267 confirms this policy, and the ghetto is born.[23]

1268 Jewry-law of Brunn is instituted: "The Jews are deprived of their natural rights and condemned to eternal misery for their sins."[24]

1272 Pope Gregory X reprimands Christians for desecrating Jewish cemeteries and hiding the bodies of their own dead children in the houses of Jews. Some Christians have done so in order to extort money by threatening to accuse the Jews of having murdered the children as part of a Passover ritual.[25]

1278 Pope Nicholas III decrees that Jews who have returned to the practice of Judaism after having been forcibly baptized must be handed over to the secular authorities, whose duty it is to burn them alive.[26]

1285 A mob in Munich accuses Jews of ritual murder and burns alive 180 Jews inside a synagogue.[27]

1290 Jews in England are reduced to a state of absolute poverty and then expelled by Edward I. They are permitted to take what property they can carry and have a military escort to their port of embarkation. Some land in Europe. One shipload is caught on the Goodwin Sands, a line of shoals at the entrance of the strait of Dover, and the passengers are put off the ship. As the tide begins to rise, the captain sails away and tells the stranded Jews to pray for help from Moses.[28]

1306 King Philip the Fair orders all one hundred thousand Jews to leave France with nothing but the clothes on their backs. Some who leave can trace their ancestry back to Jews who settled in France before the birth of Christ.[29]

1348 The plague, which is eventually to kill perhaps a third of Europe's population, strikes France. Jews are accused of poisoning the wells in Narbonne and Carcassonne. They are dragged from their homes and thrown into bonfires.[30]

1349 The entire Jewish community of Basel is burned alive in a wooden house constructed for that purpose. A decree is passed that no Jew shall be allowed to settle in Basel for two hundred years.

The two thousand Jews of Strasbourg are taken to the burial ground. All who refuse conversion are burned alive at rows of stakes. Six thousand Jews perish in Mainz, three thousand in Erfurt. All the Jews in Antwerp and Brussels are exterminated.[31]

1389 A Jewish child throws a stone at a priest leading a procession through the Jewish quarter of Prague on Easter. The townspeople proceed to slaughter three thousand Jews. When those who survive seek justice from "good

King Wenceslas," he declares that they deserve the punishment and fines the survivors instead of the murderers.[32]

1391 Fifty-thousand Jews are slaughtered in Spain because they refuse to convert to Christianity and because the Spanish clergy and nobility are short of funds.[33]

1415 Pope Benedict XII decrees that all Jews above twelve years of age shall be compelled to listen to three sermons a year. Each sermon shall demonstrate to the Jews (1) that the Messiah has already come, (2) that the "heresies, vanities and errors" of the Talmud prevent them from seeing the truth, and (3) that the destruction of the temple and their perpetual captivity were ordained by Jesus Christ.[34]

1453 St. John of Capistrano organizes drives to convert Jews in Breslau, Poland. In the process, some Jews are accused of stealing consecrated communion bread. As a result, a Jewish woman is torn apart with red-hot pincers and forty-one Jews are burned alive.[35]

1492 Torquemada, leader of the Spanish Inquisition, orders the whole Jewish population—between two hundred thousand and one million—to leave Spain on four month's notice.[36]

1496 King Manuel of Portugal orders all Jews and Moors to leave the country. The property of the Jews is confiscated and their children forcibly baptized. The Moors are spared for fear of reprisals from the Turkish and Saracen armies.[37]

1543 In his work *Concerning the Jews and Their Lies*, Martin Luther makes the following recommendations about "this damned rejected race":

> First, their synagogues or churches should be set on fire, and whatever does not burn should be covered or spread over with dirt. . . .
>
> Secondly, their home should likewise be broken down and destroyed. For they perpetrate the same things there that they do in their synagogues:
>
> Thirdly, they should be deprived of their prayer-books and Talmuds in which such idolatry, lies, cursing and blasphemy are taught.
>
> Fourthly, their rabbis must be forbidden under threat of death to teach any more. . . .
>
> Fifthly, passport and travel privileges should be absolutely forbidden to the Jews. . . .
>
> Sixthly, they ought to be stopped from usury [*usury* means any degree of interest, not only an exorbitant rate]. All their cash and valuables of silver and gold ought to be taken from them and put aside for safe keeping. . . .
>
> Seventhly, let the young and strong Jews and Jewesses be given the flail, the ax, the hoe, the spade, the distaff and spindle, and let them earn their bread by the sweat of their noses as is enjoined upon Adam's children.[38]

1555 Pope Paul IV issues a papal bull which states that the Jewish people have been condemned by God to "eternal slavery," so they should not be permitted to live among nor employ Christians, nor possess property.[39]

1565 The Council of Milan recommends a boycott of Jewish trade. It forbids Jews from practicing medicine, teaching in universities, or holding any public office that gives them authority over Christians. Sexual relations between Jews and Christians are to be considered a form of bestiality.[40]

1648 Cossack hordes occupy Homel in the Ukraine and kill two thousand Jewish men, women, and children. The same Cossacks kill two thousand Jews and six hundred Polish Catholics in Tulczyn, Polish Ukraine.[41]

1658 Oliver Cromwell attempts to legalize the return of Jews to England and meets with much opposition on religious and economic grounds. William Prynne, a Puritan pamphleteer, opposes it by declaring that Jews when allowed to live in England "crucified three or four children at least."[42]

1729 Pope Benedict XII repeats a ruling of Paul IV that forbids Christians to address Jews with terms of respect.[43]

1747 In Saslav, Poland, Jews are tortured to death as part of a ritual murder accusation.[44]

1753 In Zhytomir, Poland, eleven Jews are flayed alive as part of a ritual murder accusation.[45]

1758 The Jews of Poland appeal to the pope for protection. Pope Clement condemns the cult of the child martyrs and affirms the falsehood of *all ritual murder accusations* for the past six hundred years.[46]

1840 Monks in a Capuchin monastery bring a ritual murder charge against the Jewish community of Damascus after one of their friars and his servant disappear. Seven Jews are arrested and two of them die under torture. Although the remaining Jews are released, they are never acquitted of the murder charge.[47]

1881-1882 The semiofficial publication of the Vatican, *La Civilta Cattolica*, publishes a series of unsigned articles stating the "facts" of Jewish ritual murder charges. Here are two excerpts:

> The practice of killing children for the Paschal Feast is now very rare in the more cultivated parts of Europe. . . . [The Jews] now have other things to think of than to make their unleavened bread with Christian blood, occupied as they are in ruling almost like kings in finance and journalism. . . .
>
> It remains therefore generally proved . . . that the sanguinary Paschal rite . . . is a general law binding on the consciences of all Hebrews to make use of the blood of a Christian child, primarily for the sanctification of their souls, and also, although secondarily, to bring shame and disgrace to Christ and to Christianity.[48]

1886 Edouard Drumont publishes *La France Juive,* which "exposes" a Jewish plot to destroy Christianity and dominate France and the rest of the world. It proves immensely popular, and a subsequent edition shows a picture of the author attacking Moses and the tablets of the Law.[49]

1893 A pamphlet on "The Ritual Murder of Simon of Trent" is distributed free in Vienna churches.[50]

1894 Captain Alfred Dreyfus, a Jewish officer in the French Army, is found guilty of selling military secrets to Germany under flimsy evidence and sentenced to life imprisonment on Devil's Island. The decision is illegally based on "secret evidence" not shown to the defense. Emile Zola writes his now-famous letter to the president of the republic, *J'accuse,* protesting the decision.[51] Edouard Drumont threatens to burn Zola at the stake; he states that Jews should be thrown into the river Seine, because "what an evil odor a roasted Jew-boy would make." A French aristocrat says she hopes that "Dreyfus might be innocent so that he would suffer more."[52]

1898 A colonel in the French military admits that he forged the "secret evidence" against Dreyfus. He commits suicide. A French paper claims he has been assassinated by Jews. Dreyfus's case is reopened, and he is again found guilty because of "extenuating circumstance."[53]

1903 *The Protocols of the Learned Elders of Zion* is forged from fictional sources and published in Russia. It "proves" that Jews and Freemasons plan to disrupt Christian civilization and jointly rule the world together. Soon it is translated into all the major European languages. In the United States, Henry Ford often quotes from the *Protocols* to convince readers of his newspaper, *The Dearborn Independent*, regarding the Jewish threat.[54]

1906 The verdict against Dreyfus is annulled. However, the official French Catholic press continues to maintain his guilt. In 1916 the bishop of Nancy implies that a belief in Dreyfuss's innocence equals apostasy.[55]

1913 Cecil Chesterton writes, "We are told that the Jews have been persecuted! Well, the Irish Catholics have been persecuted . . . more severely than the Jews.[56]

1920 G. K. Chesterton condones the killing of the Jews in the First Crusade (see 1096) as "a form of democratic violence" and expresses regret that the killers cannot be canonized.[57]

1934 The historian Cecil Roth writes,

> Nazi propaganda in Germany issued periodical warnings to the general population to take special care of their children at Passover time in view of Jewish ritual requirements: and it would not be surprising if semi-official en-

> couragement were to bring about in that country, in the near future, a major tragedy reminiscent of the Middle Ages at their worst.[58]

From history, we know that Roth underestimated the Nazis.

• • •

What is known about nine centuries of abuse from Christendom against the Jewish people can only be sketchily summarized here. Hay's book has 315 pages, and I am sure that books published since on the topic are even longer. I have not touched on anti-Semitism in the United States, nor have I touched on the millions of pages of data obligingly left behind by the Nazis to document their systematic extermination of the Jewish people.

We all know what happened after Hitler came to power. Yet we need to understand that the Nazis' hatred of the Jews did not occur in a vacuum. The German people had been primed by nineteen centuries of rhetoric that came largely from the writings of the church.

Adolf Hitler himself said in an interview with a German Catholic bishop:

> As for the Jews, I am just carrying on with the same policy which the Catholic church has adopted for fifteen hundred years, when it has regarded the Jews as dangerous and pushed them into ghettos, etc., because it knew what the Jews were like. I don't put race above religion, but I do see the dangers in the representatives of this race for the Church and State, and perhaps I am doing Christianity a great service.[59]

The majority of German Christians jumped on the Nazi bandwagon without much persuasion or reflection. The Allies had shown little mercy to the German people after their defeat in World War I. Hitler came along and told them that Germans, with their superior genetic make-up, ought to rule the world and had only been prevented from doing so through an international Jewish conspiracy. He found an appreciative audience among all Germans—Christians included.

The Lutheran church leader Otto Dibelius, who later resisted the Nazis, wrote the following letter to clergy in his diocese in 1928, long before the Nazis had solidified their hold on power:

> My dear brothers,
>
> We will all have not only understanding but also full sympathy for the final motives which have given rise to the nationalist movement. Despite the ugly sound which has often attached itself to the word, I have always regarded myself as an anti-Semite. The fact cannot be concealed that the Jews have played a leading part in all the symptoms of disintegration in modern civilization. . . . May God bless our Easter and our Easter message,
>
> With heartfelt greetings, yours truly,
>
> Dibelius[60]

German Christians who put faith in the Nazi movement found that faith betrayed as the Nazis became more powerful. It soon became evident that the Nazi hierarchy felt nothing but contempt for Christianity. They consulted the churches and curried favor only so long as the churches helped them to realize their political ends. When their power was secure, they began to strip the churches of their influence, forbidding religious gatherings outside of Sunday services and shutting down religious publications. The official Nazi press regularly wrote degrading and slanderous propaganda about the German clergy—including clergy who had initially supported Hitler.

The Nazis staked out the minds and hearts of the German youth as their own territory. They gradually began closing down Christian youth organizations, and pushed young people into the ranks of the Hitler Youth.

The notes of an Austrian Hitler Youth recruitment speech survived the war. The speaker made fifty points to discredit Christianity, including the following:

> 1. Christianity is a religion for slaves and idiots, for 'The last shall be first and the first last.'. . . 'Blessed are the poor in spirit.'
>
> 3. According to Christianity, Negroes and Germans are equal.
>
> 4. The Church is international.
>
> 7. Before Christianity, German culture was at a high level, which was destroyed only by Christianity.
>
> 10. The Bible is the continuation of the Talmud, which is purely a Jewish composition. Especially the Old Testament.
>
> 18. Christianity corrupted the Germans because it introduced the ideas of adultery and theft hitherto unknown.
>
> 21. Jesus was a Jew.
>
> 23. How Christ dies (whimpering on a cross) . . .
>
> 26. The Ten Commandments are the depository of the lowest human instincts.
>
> 27. A universal Messianic idea could only be found in an inferior people; a pure race has no need of a Redeemer.
>
> 48. For us Germans, the inactivity of eternal life is foolishness.
>
> 50. Predestination, rites of the Church, the divine Trinity, original sin, etc.—what bosh![61]

The casualties of the Third Reich extend far beyond the subjugation of the German and Austrian churches, of course. The triumph of Adolf Hitler in 1933 released a storm of anti-Semitic propaganda and violence that reached terrifying depths of depravity in Germany and aroused a worldwide anti-Jewish movement unequalled in modern history. Anti-Semitism, already deeply rooted in France, was spread by the Cagoulards (French: Hooded Men). The Arrow Cross promoted it in Hungary, the British Union of Fascists in England, and the German-American Bund and the Silver Shirts in the United States. Its consequences continue to shape human history.

How This Relates to the Pharisees

It is convenient to view the Nazi era as a historical aberration. We have seen where anti-Semitism leads and feel comfortable that we have learned from history. We feel only contempt for the Ku Klux Klan and the neo-Nazis and believe that as Christians and educated people, we will not let maniacs like them ever come into power. We believe that anti-Semitism is on the wane.

I would like to believe these myths myself. And yet, over and over again, I see the passages regarding the Pharisees in the New Testament used by well-meaning and well-educated Christians as "proof" that Jesus rejected Judaism. I hear people casually referring to the legalism of Judaism without the first understanding of what the Law means to observant Jews, indeed, what the Law meant to Jesus and Paul themselves.

When we casually stereotype Judaism, based on other people's interpretations of the New Testament, we become anti-Semitic, and this anti-Semitism is insidious. It crops up in our sermons, in our Bible studies, in our denominational publications.

It can appear even in our choice of Bibles. *The Living Bible*, popular with many Christians, is a work of theology, not a translation. More specifically, it reflects Kenneth Taylor's theology.[62] Its preface clearly says that "when the Greek or Hebrew is not clear, then the theology of the translator is his guide, along with his sense of logic. . . .

The theological lodestar in this book has been a rigid evangelical position." Taylor knew no Hebrew or Greek when he set out to paraphrase the Bible, and it shows. Scholars have expressed concern about *The Living Bible's* lack of consistency when rendering parallel passages in the New Testament, its tendency at times to elaborate on a verse, inserting ideas not present in the text, and its tendency to turn ancient Hebrew or Greek phrases and technical terms into modern religious jargon.[63]

Our main concern, however, is with the blatant and subtle anti-Semitism in *The Living Bible*. For example, in the places where Jesus uses the Greek word translated by other versions as "generation," *The Living Bible* curiously uses the word "nation." Thus when Jesus speaks of an "evil and adulterous generation," in Matthew 16:4 and 12:39, *The Living Bible* causes Jesus to indict the Jewish nation rather than his contemporaries, as is clearly intended by the Greek. The difference may be subtle, but it is important when gauging subconscious anti-Semitism.

In general, Taylor grossly oversimplifies Paul's references to Judaism. He goes out of his way to indict the "legalism" of Judaism, even when Paul does not mention it. For example, he paraphrases Galatians 4:3 ("enslaved to the elemental spirits of the world,") as "slaves to Jewish laws and rituals." In Galatians 4:9, "weak and beggarly elemental spirits" becomes "another poor, weak useless religion of trying to get to heaven by obeying God's laws."

To describe the Pharisees, *The Living Bible* adds negative adjectives that do not appear in the Greek. Consider the Scriptures that we examined in chapter 4. Compare, for example, the parable of the Pharisee and the tax collector as translated by the *New Revised Standard Version* and paraphrased by *The Living Bible:*

NRSV

Luke 18:[9]He also told this parable to some who trusted in themselves that they were righteous and regarded others with contempt: [10]"Two men went up to the temple to pray, one a Pharisee and the other a tax collector. [11]The Pharisee, standing by himself, was praying thus, 'God, I thank you that I am not like other people: thieves, rogues, adulterers, or even like this tax collector. [12]I fast twice a week; I give a tenth of all my income.' [13]But the tax collector, standing far off, would not even look up to heaven, but was beating his breast and saying, 'God, be merciful to me, a sinner!' [14]I tell you, this man went down to his home justified rather than the other; for all who exalt themselves will be humbled, but all who humble themselves will be exalted."

The Living Bible

Luke 18:[9]Then he told this story to some who boasted of their virtue and scorned everyone else:

[10]"Two men went to the Temple to pray. One was a proud, self-righteous Pharisee, and the other a cheating tax collector. [11]The proud Pharisee 'prayed' this prayer: 'Thank God, I am not a sinner like everyone else, especially like that tax collector over there! For I never cheat, I don't commit adultery, [12]I go without food twice a week, and I give to God a tenth of everything I earn.'

[13]"But the corrupt tax collector stood at a distance and dared not even lift his eyes to heaven as he prayed, but beat upon his chest in sorrow, exclaiming, 'God, be merciful to me, a sinner.' [14]I tell you, this sinner, not the Pharisee, returned home forgiven! For the proud shall be humbled, but the humble shall be honored."

Notice that *The Living Bible* inserts the words "proud" and "self-righteous" in verse 10 although the Greek merely uses the word "Pharisee." In verse 11, the word "proud" also is inserted. Also, in verse 11, it puts the word "prayed" in quotations, as if to imply that the Pharisee was not really doing so. The message of the prayer is radically altered in

The Living Bible. In the Greek, the Pharisee says that he is not a thief, rogue, or adulterer. He never claims he does not sin. Yet *The Living Bible* puts words in his mouth to make him claim to be sinless.

We do not have time or space to compare *The Living Bible's* version of Matthew 23 with a reputable translation, but it is worthwhile comparing the first three verses of that chapter.

NRSV

Matthew 23:[1]Then Jesus said to the crowds and to his disciples, [2]"The scribes and the Pharisees sit on Moses' seat; [3]therefore, do whatever they teach you and follow it; but do not do as they do, for they do not practice what they teach.

The Living Bible

Matthew 23:[1]Then Jesus said to the crowds, and to his disciples, [2]"You would think these Jewish leaders and these Pharisees were Moses, the way they keep making up so many laws!" [3]And of course you should obey their every whim! It may be all right to do what they say, but above anything else, *don't follow their example.* For they don't do what they tell you to do.

The reference to Moses' seat, as was mentioned in chapter 4, is a bit obscure in the Greek, but likely refers to a teaching role in the synagogue. The sense of the passage is that since the scribes and Pharisees have studied the laws of Moses, people should listen to their teachings, but should not necessarily do what they do.

In adding his own words to these verses, Taylor distorts the meaning of the passage. The Greek says nothing about the scribes and Pharisees pretending they are Moses, neither does the Greek say anything at all about the Pharisees "making up so many laws." The simple declarative sentence, "Therefore do whatever they teach you," becomes padded beyond recognition. "And of course you should obey their every whim!" is a sentence purely of

Taylor's creation, with no corresponding sentence in the Greek, and the added exclamation point makes it seem ironic rather than straightforward. Instead of saying that his listeners should do what the Pharisees teach, the Jesus of *The Living Bible* grudgingly presents it as an option. "But above everything else" is another Taylor tack-on.

Some may argue that Kenneth Taylor had a right to interpret the Bible as he wishes, since he admits his work is a paraphrase. For the purposes of unearthing the anti-Semitism in our religious life, however, we should prayerfully consider whether it is appropriate to use a paraphrase that heaps insults on Pharisees and Jews in general. Christians have used Jesus' words on the Pharisees for centuries to persecute Jews, not understanding that Jesus, a Jew, spoke to the religious establishment of his day—just as he would have spoken to the religious establishment of our day. In putting additional anti-Jewish propaganda into Jesus' mouth, *The Living Bible* takes enormous liberties with the text of the Scriptures and fuels anti-Semitism in its readers.

The fires of anti-Semitism in the church have burned quite long enough.

Conclusion

I challenge the reader to become more aware about casual references to Judaism and Pharisaism in religious life. There are good reasons for us to make this effort.

First, it is the right thing to do. As Bible-believing Christians, we are responsible to put the text of Scripture above our own historical prejudices. Because Christians have used God's Word to humiliate, ostracize, and murder Jews, we have the obligation to use our knowledge of Scripture redemptively, to include rather than to exclude, to feed our love instead of our hate.

Second, we need to become aware of the church's history of anti-Semitism for reasons of self-preservation. We do not want to get caught unawares, as most of the German Christians were, if another malevolent political force arises that consolidates its power through the hatred of a particular group of people. If the church is living faithfully, any political power founded on hate will inevitably turn against the church. Maurice Samuel wrote in 1940,

> We shall never understand the maniacal, world-wide seizure of anti-Semitism unless we transpose the terms. It is of Christ that the Nazi-fascists are afraid; it is in his omnipotence that they believe; it is him they are determined madly to obliterate. . . . They must spit on the Jews as "the Christ-killers" because they long to spit on the Jews as the Christ-givers.[64]

Those living in the love of Christ must always present a target for those living in hate.

Finally, I believe that if we refuse to acknowledge the church's history of anti-Semitism and our own anti-Semitism, we will never successfully climb the wall that stands between Jews and Christians. I believe that we owe it to God and to ourselves to engage in dialogue with Jewish believers, not just because it will enrich us, but because there are serious issues that we need to tackle together.

For example, until we understand our horrible history of persecuting the Jews, we cannot really talk with each other on issues surrounding the state of Israel and Israeli-Palestinian relationships.[65] Some of my friends have expressed impatience with the way Jews "use" their past persecutions in order to justify Israeli policies. One of my professors went so far as to say he refuses to listen any more to stories of the Holocaust, because he is so appalled by Israeli military policy.

I believe that this is the wrong approach. As long as we refuse to listen to the Jews regarding their history, the Jews have every right to refuse to listen to us. We need to understand why Jews throughout the world crave the security that came with the founding of the state of Israel. We need to acknowledge they have every right to be afraid, given the way society has persecuted their ancestors for nearly two millennia.

Consider the following statement by the theologian Emil Fackenheim,

> Few Jews are indifferent to the plight of the Arab refugees. For my part, I cannot deny the Palestinian Arabs the right to a state of their own that I claim for my people. What fills me with frustration bordering on despair—and indeed with doubt whether, after all, such a thing as Jewish-Christian dialogue is possible—is any Christian view that the survival of the Jewish state is a "merely political" matter to which I must be "religiously" indifferent if I am to be a worthy partner in Jewish-Christian dialogue. Do Christians think that Judaism could survive a second Holocaust—or that Israel could survive without her army? Are they to have dialogue with dead Jews?[66]

It is insensitive and unchristian to disregard Jewish fears. If we accuse Jews of paranoia, that will effectively squelch any meaningful conversation over issues of peace and justice in the Middle East. We cannot speak prophetically about oppression of the Palestinians until we humbly and mournfully acknowledge Christianity's history of oppressing the Jews.

For Discussion

1. When did you first understand how many people had been killed by the Nazis? How did you react? Has the Holocaust had any effect on the way you view God?

2. How responsible do you feel for the church's historic persecution of the Jews?

3. Gerhard Kittel was one of the more famous German theologians who supported Hitler. He even wrote propaganda for the Nazi Party, although he claimed later in his defense that his anti-Semitism was based purely on religious grounds rather than racial grounds. After the war, in defense of his efforts on behalf of the Nazis, he wrote,

> Never has a more terrible judgment been spoken against the so-called world Jewry as a demand for power than in the 'woe' of Jesus Christ in Matthew 23:15; never a more negative characterization of the Jewish religion as a religion of privilege than that found in John 8:40-44![67]

Knowing what you do about the Pharisees and Judaism in general during the life of Christ, how would you respond to Kittel?

4. A few years ago, I was reading some memoirs written by my grandfather. He was a gentle and decent man who loved Christ and the church. I was startled when I came to a section from his boyhood where he described his father dickering with another man over the price of some livestock. My grandfather said that his father tried to "jew him down."

Can you think of subtle and perhaps subconscious ways that anti-Semitism has affected your life?

7

Toward Humility and Dialogue

A. Mennonites/Amish	1. Can refer to a culture, ethnic identity, as well as a religion.
B. Jews	2. Members are divided between various factions, some more liberal, some more conservative.
C. Nuns/Monks	3. Members of more conservative factions wear traditional clothing.
D. Hutterites	4. Emphasize separation from society as part of religious belief.
E. Jehovah's Witnesses	5. Have experienced persecution as a result of their faith. Their history of persecution has deeply influenced their theology.

On the previous page, try to match each group with a descriptive statement.

• • •

Deuteronomy 5:9-10 reads,

> You shall not bow down to them or worship them; for I the Lord your God am a jealous God, punishing children for the iniquity of parents, to the third and fourth generation of those who reject me, [10]but showing steadfast love to the thousandth generation of those who love me and keep my commandments.

Many people who think of the God of the Old Testament as a stern and punishing God often use Deuteronomy 5:9 to prove their position. After all, it doesn't seem fair that God would punish the children of people who rejected God.

In the ancient Hebrew worldview, people believed that God caused everything to happen, good and bad. When they observed the way their society functioned and how children grew up and the events that occurred in their community, they did not ask, "What happened?" but rather "Why did God make this happen?"[1]

Thus, Deuteronomy 5:9 says more about the nature of humanity than it does about the nature of God. The consequences of parents rejecting God's commandments will likely be passed to their children and grandchildren. Ezekiel 18:2 refers to this theme by quoting the ancient proverb, "The parents have eaten sour grapes, and the children's teeth are set on edge."

This proverb holds true today. Alcoholism runs in families. So does child abuse. A sour relationship with one's father may have its roots in the abusive behavior of a great-great-grandparent.

If I elaborated on Deuteronomy 5:9, I would say that

the worst social evils visit themselves on people for much longer than four generations.

Take, for example, more than two centuries of slavery in the United States and race relations in that country today. Despite legal precedents that dictate that people of all races should be treated equally, we live in hatred or suspicion of each other. When people of good will wish to reach out to each other, they find their advances stymied by people who do not want dialogue, who prefer to live comfortably with their prejudices and don't want a bunch of "do-gooders" spoiling their comfort.

I believe we need to keep Deuteronomy 5:9 and Ezekiel 18:2 in mind when we speak about the need for Jewish-Christian dialogue. We cannot erase nearly two millennia of inflammatory rhetoric, persecution, and murder. Nor should we. Our desire to enter into dialogue with Jews, should at least come in part from our desire to make things right. And we cannot do so without taking the past into account.

How then can we get beyond the wall of mistrust that separates us? We need to acknowledge from the outset that we may not be able to do this. Many religious Jews, with whom we would most desire to come to an understanding, long ago gave up the idea of true dialogue.

In 1966, Eliezer Berkovits, professor at Hebrew Theological College in Skokie, Illinois, wrote that he viewed overtures by Christians to establish interreligious dialogue as ethically objectionable. He said that doing so falsifies historical truth in that it implies mutual responsibility for the friction in Jewish-Christian relations. To speak of "conflicts" whitewashes the fact that Christians unilaterally oppressed the Jews for centuries. Furthermore, Berkovits writes, respect for another person should not be made dependent on whether one can appreciate the other's theology. We have the duty to respect each other regardless of religious beliefs.

"It is not a matter of whether Christianity acknowledges fragmentary truths in Judaism," writes Berkovits. "All we want of Christians is that they keep their hands off us and our children!"[2]

Religious Jews do not universally share Berkovits's objection to dialogue, but his views are not rare, either. Bearing this in mind, I believe that the only way Christians who wish to establish dialogue can do so is to approach it from a standpoint of extreme humility. I believe we cannot come to this standpoint without accepting responsibility for past and present injustices.

We may rebel at the thought of identifying ourselves with the inquisitors of the Middle Ages and the Nazis. We would like to think we would have hidden Jews in our basements in Nazi-occupied Europe. We may not consider ourselves anti-Semites today. Fine. But taking a defensive posture will not facilitate dialogue. If we truly wish to create right relationships with the Jewish people, we must make ourselves vulnerable and admit that the Christian religion that has nourished and sustained us is the same religion that Christians have used to persecute and kill the Jews.

We may not be the type of person who would deliberately exclude Jews from the country club. We might scorn the idea of belonging to a country club in the first place. The fact that we could belong to a country club if we wanted to, however, binds us to the anti-Semites who would keep Jews and other minorities out whether we like it or not. I believe that the only way we can break this bond is through accepting responsibility for their anti-Semitism. Jesus Christ set a precedent, after all, when he took upon himself the sins of others. He made himself vulnerable to attack for the sake of reconciling people to God. We need to follow his example if we want to reconcile with each other.

We also need to have the humility to change our thinking. Rosemary Ruether, in her provocative book, *Faith and Fratricide,* has suggested the following changes in curriculum for theological schools and seminaries:

1. Christian biblical scholars must study the Talmud's commentary and interpretation of the Hebrew Scriptures. In doing so, they may be less likely to assign the Hebrew Scriptures to the status of "Old Testament" and to believe that the advent of Christianity made Judaism obsolete.

2. New Testament scholars should put the thought of Jesus and Paul into a rabbinic context. That is, they should view their thought in the light of other Jewish teachers living around the same time whose teachings appear in the Talmud. Christians need to grapple with the "anti-Jewish" (as distinguished from anti-Semitic) writings in the New Testament and seek ways of overcoming them when preparing people to preach.

3. Church historians should teach the history of Christendom's persecution of the Jews by religious and political rulers. They need to make Christians aware of Christianity's responsibility for "the translation of theological anti-Judaism into social anti-Semitism."

4. Christian theologians must question the anti-Judaic thinking that has stemmed from our understanding of redemption. They need to think of ways to eliminate this thinking in their interpretation of the gospel.

5. Christian seminaries should cultivate face-to-face conversation between their faculty and students, and religious Jews. Christians need to become aware of the conflict between the way we perceive the "Jewish-Christian tradition" and the Jewish historical perspective. Field education courses for pastors should include contact with local rabbis and Jewish community agencies.

6. Courses in preaching and Christian education must eliminate anti-Judaic language in biblical interpretation and educational and liturgical materials.[3]

Since the appearance of Ruether's book in 1974, I believe that the curriculum in many theological schools has undergone a change which reflects some of these suggestions. However, I still hear sermons preached about villainous Pharisees. Most of the people who have asked about this book expressed genuine surprise when I told them that the Pharisees paralleled the good "churchgoing" people of our own time.

Therefore, I believe that Christian lay people must take upon themselves the task of revising the stereotypes we have acquired of Pharisees and Judaism in general.

Michael Cook, a Jewish New Testament scholar, compiled a list of ten stereotypes which have resulted from Christian writers misinterpreting the New Testament.[4] Where necessary, I have included my own comments in parentheses.

1. The Jews are responsible for crucifying Jesus. (Chapter 3 in this book showed that the four Gospels differ in their accounts of how much responsibility some of the Jewish *leaders* had for Christ's death. In any case, crucifixion was a purely Roman form of execution.)

2. The sufferings of the Jewish people are a result of God's punishment for their killing Jesus. (See above.)

3. Jesus originally came to preach only to the Jews; when they rejected him, he urged that they be abandoned in favor of the Gentiles. (As we know, the people who *accepted* Jesus were also Jews, as were the majority of the earliest Christians.)

4. The children of Israel were God's original chosen people by virtue of an ancient covenant. By rejecting Jesus, the Jews forfeited their chosenness. Now, by virtue of a new covenant, Christians have replaced Jews as God's chosen people. (See above.)

5. The Jewish Bible repeatedly portrays the opaqueness

and stubbornness of the Jewish people and their faithlessness to God. (Yes, but it also shows their faithfulness in the face of oppression and exile. The prophets were all Jews, as were King David, Ezra, Nehemiah, and most other leaders named. Some Jews in the Old Testament were faithful, some weren't. Again, we are dealing with human nature. We can just as easily say that Paul's letters show the "opaqueness and stubbornness" of all the early Christians if we cited some of his admonitions in his letters to the Galatians and Corinthians.)

6. The Jewish Bible is filled with predictions of the coming of Jesus as the Messiah, yet the Jews are blind to the meaning of their own Scripture (This is a sticky one. It presents issues much too large for the scope of this book. I would say, however, that although the writers of the Gospels did interpret some of Hebrew Scripture to indicate the coming Christ, later Christian writers went to an extreme in their use of allegory to find such prophecies. Many Christian writers have erred greatly in assuming that everything in the Hebrew Bible points to the coming of Jesus, from the rivers named in Genesis 2:10-14 to the erotic poetry in the Song of Songs.)

7. By the time of Jesus' ministry, Judaism ceased to be a living faith. (But Jesus' ministry was a *part* of the living faith of Judaism. The synagogues and temples today testify to the fact that Judaism continues as a living faith.)

8. The essence of Judaism is a restrictive and burdensome legalism. (Do we really need to reiterate that the essence of all religions can—and usually does—become so?)

9. The New Testament religion (Christianity) emphasizes love; the Jewish Bible emphasizes legalism, justice, and a God of wrath. (Read John 3:36; Rom. 2:5-8; Rev. 14:7-20. Then read Exod. 34:6; Lev. 19:34; Ps. 36:7; Isa. 54:10. Better yet, get a good concordance and look up "wrath," "anger," "love," "compassion," and so on. You will find the words well distributed throughout both Testaments.)

10. The oppressive legalism of Judaism reflects the disposition of Jesus' opponents called "Pharisees"; in their teachings as well as their behavior, the Pharisees were all hypocrites. (I know you know better.)

By now, you may begin to feel uneasy because of what is being asked of you. You may have been fully prepared to renounce anti-Semitism and take responsibility for the injustices Christianity has perpetrated on Judaism. But what about John 3:16? Are we not compromising our Christianity if we do not insist that Jesus Christ is the only way, the only truth, and the only life? Is not Christianity, in its very essence, an evangelical religion? If we truly believe that salvation comes through Jesus Christ alone, are we not shirking our duty if we do not witness to everyone, including the Jews?

I believe these questions are beyond the scope of this book, just as are the difficult religious and political issues from the Middle East. However, I do not call for us to ignore these issues or avoid the controversy surrounding them. Instead, I advocate discussing these issues from a position of extreme humility.

Part of this humility involves eliminating offensive Christian stereotypes of Judaism. Only when we have done so can we move on to the final step which makes for good dialogue. That step is identification. This book set out to help readers identify with the humanity of the Pharisees. In doing so, we can easily identify with the humanity of their spiritual descendants.

Identification does not mean putting aside our religious differences and looking for some spiritual lowest common denominator as a compromise. Indeed, it means rather the opposite. It means acknowledging that some people who love God with all their heart, mind, and soul are channeling such spirituality in ways that seem foreign to us. Identification means being able to see the love.

I joined the Mennonite Church when I was nineteen and felt a sense of having come home at last. The Mennonite Church has nurtured me and challenged me and helped me to grow. That being said, I have always felt more of a kinship with devout Catholics and Jews than I have with secular Mennonites—those who have a strong attachment to the ethnic and cultural aspects but not to the theological aspects of being a Mennonite. I find that I identify more easily with people who come from a denomination with a strong sense of identity, such as the Christian Reformed, than I do with those who come from some of the larger mainstream denominations.

Finding it easier to identify with devout Jews than apathetic Christians is not the paradox it may appear to some people. Abraham Heschel once said, "The first and most important prerequisite of interfaith is faith." [5]

If we do not have a commitment to our own faith, we cannot really understand people who have a commitment to a different faith. Therefore, loving Jesus Christ with our heart, soul, and mind will make it easier for us to identify with religious Jews.

Such identification could take place on several levels. For example, having heard Catholics talk about their mothers, I have come to the conclusion that Jewish mothers are not the only ones who parent aggressively (and was that stereotype ever really true?). On a much deeper level, Catholics ought to be able to identify with Judaism on the basis of the liturgical style of worship and the importance of the family unit in their religions. Christians belonging to the Reformed tradition could relate to Judaism on the importance of covenant and the centrality of Scripture in their theologies.

Between my own Anabaptist theology and tradition

and those of Judaism, I see several parallels. Both Jews and Anabaptists take a radically obedient approach to Scripture. Both have histories of persecution as a result of this radical interpretation of Scripture. Both have a history of separation from mainstream society built into their religious beliefs.

One of the driving forces behind this book has been this question: Since Anabaptists and Jews were persecuted, killed, and exiled in Europe around the same times and in some of the same places, by the same people, and for some of the same reasons, why didn't they join forces? Why didn't they reach out to help and comfort each other?

I have seen the pictures in *The Martyrs Mirror*[6] of Anabaptists being tortured, dismembered, and burned at the stake. I have heard the stories of older Mennonites and their children who escaped from the Ukraine in the early part of this century after pogroms destroyed Mennonite villages, killing whole families. Barbara Claassen Smucker, who wrote the children's book, *Days of Terror*,[7] about this period in Mennonite history, once told me that a Jewish acquaintance had read it and marveled at how similar the story was to what his own family had suffered in the Ukraine.

So why, I wondered, hadn't Mennonites and Jews heard of each other's sufferings? Why, in my search of both Jewish and Mennonite resources, could I find such scant evidence for any Anabaptist-Jewish dialogue?

The conclusions I came to are hypothetical—and sobering. On a benign level, I believe that their shared emphasis on separation from society and its values served to separate the Anabaptists and the Jews. In the Ukraine, Mennonite and Jewish settlements were sufficiently far apart and isolationist to prevent much contact between the two groups during the pogroms in the teens and twenties. Also, I think both groups were caught up enough in their own problems that they did not have time to worry about the suffering of others.

On a tragic level, I have come to believe that the early Anabaptists and later the Mennonites, nurtured on the same Jewish myths as the rest of Christendom, were probably as anti-Semitic as other Christians of their times. I would like to think that their philosophy of nonviolence prevented most of them from physically harming Jews, but they probably thought of them as Christ-killers like all the good Catholics and Protestants.

When I went to the Mennonite Historical Library at my alma mater to look up examples of Mennonite-Jewish encounters, I found only arcane pieces of information that did not really speak to the purpose of this study. (For example, did you know that Spinoza, after being condemned as a heretic by his Jewish community in the seventeenth century, found refuge with the Mennonites in Holland?) A volunteer in the Mennonite Historical Library told me he had worked for a Dutch Mennonite scholar, Frits Kuiper, who had written about Jewish-Christian dialogue, but none of his works had been translated into English.[8]

Mostly I turned up pamphlets and books written by Mennonites on how to win Jews to Christ. I found particularly discouraging one book on this theme that had a section subtitled, "The Psychology of Suppressed Minorities." It went into detail about the "neuroses" and "character defects" of the Jews without once stopping to make a connection between the neuroses and character defects of the many Mennonites who will never live completely without fear or sadness as a result of the persecution they have suffered.

Of course, there may be untold accounts of Jews preserved by Mennonites in times of persecution, and vice versa. One such story came from Zev Garber, a Jewish scholar on the *Sho'ah* (Holocaust), of Van Nuys, California.

During a time of pogroms in Russia, his forebear was given refuge in a Mennonite home and there obtained his Swiss-German name of Gerber/Garber.[9] However, such reports are anecdotal and isolated.

When I call other Christians to an attitude of extreme humility in our relationship to Judaism, it is because I find that I need to cultivate this attitude myself. I remember in seminary how it used to annoy me that students from various Baptist denominations traced their roots back to the Anabaptist movement. I believe the historical connection to be tenuous, but my objection sprang more from emotional reasons. I was offended that Baptists claimed the Anabaptist movement as their own and romanticized the sufferings of the early Anabaptists without adopting the pacifism and separation from the state integral to the Anabaptist movement.

Yet, in a sense, I had done the same thing by identifying the sufferings by my church with that of the Jews throughout history. While Anabaptists were reviled by the authorities for their theology, they were never viewed as innately disgusting, abhorrent, and even foul smelling by the mass of Christendom.[10] In general, the Anabaptists mostly had to fear the civil authorities, while the Jews had to live in constant wariness for mob violence. The Mennonites often had the option of emigrating to avoid execution—an option denied to many Jews.

It was presumptuous of me to think that my church was somehow less at fault for hatred of the Jews than other churches. Somehow, in my desire to connect Anabaptist and Jewish experiences, I forgot the story told me by one of my old pastors of how he received permission to visit German Mennonite prisoners of war captured by the allies in World War II.

"How could you fight for Hitler, when you saw what he was doing to the Jews?" he asked them.

"Hitler was against communism" was their only justification.

I forgot that when the Nazi armies invaded the Ukraine in 1941, they slaughtered the Jewish villages and caused great suffering for the native Russians, but accorded special privileges to Mennonites as a German-speaking people.[11] I forgot that many of the casual condemnations of the Old Testament, Pharisees, and Judaism that prompted this book came from Mennonite lips.

So it is with humility that I still encourage Mennonites to reach out to Jews when they have the opportunity, to ask forgiveness for blatant and subtle anti-Semitism, and to seek ways of identifying with the Jewish experience. I believe besides being the right thing to do, it will enrich us and give us a deeper understanding of the historical dynamics that have affected us. I believe it will enable us to develop a distinctly Anabaptist view of the Scriptures,[12] and I believe it will make us a more decent, compassionate people.

A Flawed Relationship

Michael Cook, a Jewish New Testament scholar, was once invited to participate in a group that had set out to eliminate anti-Jewish rhetoric in the New Testament. He declined and offered as an alternative to this group an oft-retold Jewish parable:

Once King Solomon gave a banquet for all the jewelers in his realm. He wanted their advice on how he might repair a beautiful diamond that had had one of its facets scratched. He asked the jewelers whether someone could erase the scratch. After they had looked at the gem, one by one they shook their heads and left.

One jeweler stayed behind to speak to the crestfallen king.

"Sire," he said, "some scratches are so deep we cannot

ever erase them, so we have to transform them the best we can." Using one of his tools, he engraved a lily on the facet, using the scratch as its stem. The diamond was never perfect again, never the flawless gem that King Solomon would have most wanted, but it was beautiful in its own way.[13]

I do not pretend that the horrors of Auschwitz can ever be made beautiful or that the memories of it will ever be more than a source of pain for humanity. However, I believe that we can redemptively use the scars left behind by five hundred generations of persecution. If they cause one Christian to begin questioning assumptions about Judaism, if they inspire one Christian to reach out to others whom society does not tolerate, if they bring one Christian to a position of abject humility—then these scars will have functioned as agents of grace. And they will have succeeded in drawing us closer to the Jewish carpenter's son we love.

Conclusion

When I first set out to tackle Christians' perceptions of Pharisees, I looked through the *Religion Index One: Periodicals* for religious and denominational magazines written for lay people. I found a short piece entitled "Clinical Notes of a Former Pharisee," included as a sidebar in a longer article written by a doctor who treats AIDS patients.

I came across his sentence, "AIDS is a disease that appeals to Pharisees." "Aha," I thought. "I can use this to show what a distorted picture most Christians have of the Pharisees. This doctor suffers under the erroneous perception that all Pharisees were self-righteous and hardhearted. I'll tear him apart."

My own self-righteous glee got cut short by what followed:

> One of my first thoughts, when I began taking care of James, was to thank God that I was not like him. And then I remembered the moral Jesus added at the end of the parable of the Pharisee and the publican: "Every one that exalteth himself shall be abased; and he that humbleth himself shall be exalted. . . .
>
> I began my treatment of James with the attitude of a Pharisee, thanking God that I was "not as other men"; I tried to see his disease as somehow different from other diseases; I did not consider the possibility that this stigmatized man had repented and had been forgiven while I was yet in my sins. In my heart, I approved of his suffering and inevitable death.
>
> I count all these sins equal to his—no, much greater, according to Jesus. . . . I feel the struggle of plague time within me, and realize the parallels between AIDS and other plagues. Then I remember the story of the Pharisee and the tax collector, the one about the self-righteous plague doctor and the homosexual AIDS patient.[14]

If I eliminated the word "former" in the title and changed the words "attitude of a Pharisee" to "attitude of the Pharisee in Luke 18:9-14," I believe that these words admirably sum up the purpose of this book.

No matter what our intentions might be, any good deed or quality almost inevitably degenerates into something petty or even wicked. Earnest desires to follow God's will in all aspects of our life can swiftly become legalistic. Desires to do the right thing become self-righteousness. Desires for purity become exclusiveness or snobbery.

We need to reread the biblical passages on the Pharisees in the light of this awareness of our own sins. We need to understand that the Pharisees did not constitute some monolithic human evil. Instead, they consisted of good and bad people in about the same percentages as any other religious group. We need to face up to the hatred and persecution that our spiritual ancestors perpetrated on the Jews in the name of Jesus Christ.

We have all sinned and fallen short of the glory of God—not because we are Pharisees, but because we are human.

For Discussion

1. How does the matching exercise at the opening of this chapter speak to similarities and differences between religious bodies? How does it speak to the nature of faith? Think of several religions and denominations familiar to you. Which are most like your own? Which are most different? What things do you hold in common with those most different?

2. How should we respond to historical evils, injustices that have already happened? How do we usually respond?

3. How does your pastor refer to Pharisees and Jews in sermons? How do you think your pastor would respond to Ruether's guidelines given in this chapter?

4. If we took a position of extreme humility, how would this affect our relationships with our family? With our friends? With people of other religions, races, cultures, etc.? How would the foreign policy of your country change if it took a position of extreme humility in its relationships with other countries?

Abila
Damascus
ABILENE
Mt. Hermon
SYRIA
Caesarea Philippi
Sidon
Zarephath
N
W
E
S
Tyre
PHOENICIA
GALILEE
Chorazin
Bethsaida
Capernaum
Ptolemais
Mt. Carmel
Magadan
Sea of Galilee
Cana
Tiberias
Nazareth
Mt. Tabor
Nain
Gadara
DECAPOLIS
Caesarea
Mediterranean Sea
Salim
Aenon
Jordan River
Gerasa
Samaria
Mt. Ebal
SAMARIA
Sychar
PEREA
Mt. Gerizim
Joppa
+Arimathea
Ephraim
Jericho
+Bethany
Emmaus
Qumran
Azotus
Jerusalem
Bethany
JUDEA
Bethlehem
Ascalon
Dead Sea
Machaerus
Gaza
Hebron
IDUMEA
NABATEA
Palestine in New Testament Times
Map by Paula Johnson, Merrill R. Miller, and Jan Gleysteen
+ Means city has uncertain location

Notes

Chapter 1: We Are the Pharisees

1. *Merriam Webster's Collegiate Dictionary*, tenth ed. (Springfield, Mass.: Merriam-Webster, 1993), 870.

2. These persecutions have occasionally happened simultaneously, like the pogroms in Russia during the first part of this century. However, the parallels are not exact, and historically the Jews have suffered longer and more extensively than members of the various Anabaptist groups. See chapter 7.

Chapter 2: First-Century Palestine

1. Post-cataclysm.

2. Anthony Saldarini writes, "In most historical reconstructions of Jewish society, the categories used to describe [Pharisees, Scribes, and Sadducees] such as sect, school, upper class, lay leadership, etc., are ill-defined or misused and not integrated into an understanding of the overall structure and functioning of society." *Pharisees, Scribes and Sadducees* (Wilmington: Michael Glazier, 1988), 3.

3. These four are basic, not absolute. Eduard Lohse divides first-century Judaism into seven different factions. In addition to Pharisees, Sadducees, and Essenes, he writes about Zealots, Theraputae, the Qumran Community, and Scribes. *The New Testament Environment* (Nashville: Abingdon Press, 1976), 74-119. There were probably many other religious and political factions of which we have no record.

4. Hebrew for "people of the land," pronounced *ahm hah-AHR-ets.*

5. Lawrence H. Schiffman, "The Significance of the Scrolls," *Bible Review* 8 (June 1992): 33, 54. See also Schiffman's essay, "Jewish Sectarianism in Second Temple Times," in *Great Schisms in Jewish History*, ed. by Raphael Jospe and Stanley M. Wagner (New York: KTAV Publishing House, 1981), 12-15; *Anchor Bible Dictionary* (ABD), 2:619-626.

6. Schiffman, "Jewish Sectarianism in Second Temple Times," 32-33; Jacob Neusner, *From Politics to Piety: The Emergence of Pharisaic Judaism* (Englewood Cliffs, New Jersey: Prentice Hall, 1973), 55.

7. Hos. 6:6 (NRSV). See also Amos 5:23-24 and Mic. 6:6-8.

8. This dating reflects scholarly consensus. However, John A. T. Robinson,

Redating the New Testament (Philadelphia: Westminster Press, 1976), argues for dating the Gospels before the fall of the temple.

9. Saldarini, 84-85.

10. Neusner, Jacob, *From Politics to Piety*, xii-xiii.

11. See 1 Maccabees 1:9-63; 2 Macc. 6.

12. Refer to map in the appendix.

13. Jacob Neusner, *From Politics to Piety*, 14.

14. Jamnia, Jabneh; Hebrew: Yabneh, Yabneel; cf. 2 Chron. 26:6; 2 Macc. 12:8-9; about twelve miles south of Joppa.

15. The Jews call this collection of scripture by the acronym *Tanakh*, made from the first letters of Torah (law), Nevi'im (prophets), and Ketuvim (Writings). This book will refer to the collection as the Hebrew Bible instead of the Old Testament, because the passage of time has not rendered it obsolete for either Christians or Jews.

16. See especially Gal. 2:7-14; 5:1-6; 6:11-15.

17. John T. Townsend, "The Gospel of John and the Jews," *Anti-Semitism and the Foundations of Christianity*, ed. Alan Davies (New York: Paulist Press 1979), 84-85. The historian Eusebius says that Jewish antagonism was fueled by the Christians' abandonment of Jerusalem when the Romans besieged and destroyed it during the first Jewish revolt, A.D. 66-70.

18. B. (Babylonian Talmud) Berakhoth 28b; from Lohse, 163.

19. B. Sanhedrin 58b-59a; from David Novak, *Jewish-Christian Dialogue: A Jewish Justification* (New York: Oxford University Press, 1989), 32.

20. T. (Babylonian Talmud) Shabbat 12 (14): 5; from Lawrence H. Schiffman, *Who Was a Jew?: Rabbinic and Halakhic Perspectives on the Jewish-Christian Schism* (Hoboken, N.J.: KTAV Publishing House, 1985), 62.

21. See Acts 9:22-23; 23:12-15.

22. See Acts 15:1-5.

23. See Rom. 9:1-3; 11:1; 2 Cor. 11:21b-22; Gal. 1:13-14; Phil. 3:4-6.

24. (Englewood Cliffs, N.J.: Prentice Hall, 1973), xix.

Chapter 3: Overlooked Pharisees

1. Cornelius J. Dyck, ed., *An Introduction to Mennonite History*, 3d ed. (Scottdale: Herald Press, 1993), pp. 102-104; ME, 3:577-584.

2. Luke 7:36-50; 11:37-41; 14:1-6.

3. Refusing to wash his hands also had ritualistic implications. Cf. Mishnah Hagigah 2.5; 3.2.

4. Viviano and Taylor, "Sadducees, Angels, and Resurrection (Acts 23:8-9)," *Journal of Biblical Literature* 111 (1992): 496; cf. Acts 4:1-2, where the Sadducees are "much annoyed" because Peter and John proclaim that "in Jesus there is the resurrection of the dead."

5. Douglas E. Oakman, *Jesus and the Economic Questions of His Day* (Lewiston, N.Y.: Edwin Mellen Press, 1986), 66-71.

6. Eduard Lohse, *The New Testament Environment* (Nashville: Abingdon, 1976), 80

7. Lohse, 121.

8. "Test"—Matt. 16:1; 19:3; 22:18, 35; Mark 8:11, 10:2; Luke 10:25, a lawyer, likely a Pharisee; 11:16, others. "Trap/entrap"—Matt. 22:15; Mark 12:13.

9. Mark 8:11||Matt. 16:1; Mark 10:2||Matt. 19:3; Mark 12:13||Matt. 22:15. Luke 11:16 refers to "others," not Pharisees.

10. Mark 2:13-18, 23-28; 3:1-6; 7:1-23; 8:11-13; 10:2; 12:13-17.

11. Luke 10:25-28; 11:14-23; 11:29-32; 20:9-19; 20:20-26; 20:41-44. It should be noted that one of the perplexing aspects of studying the references to Pharisees in the synoptic Gospels is that none of them consistently villainizes the Pharisees. Hence, in parallel stories, Mark may refer to scribes or lawyers when Matthew refers to Pharisees and vice versa. See Saldarini, p. 158.

12. Pheme Perkins notes in *Resurrection: New Testament Witness and Contemporary Reflection* (Garden City, N.Y.: Doubleday, 1984), 161-162, that meals play an important part in the Lukan narrative. "These meals tie together Jesus's earthly ministry, the period of the resurrected One's appearances to the disciples, and the eucharistic experiences of the Lukan Christians."

13. Donald Cook, "A Gospel Portrait of the Pharisees," *Review and Expositor* 84:232-233.

14. John T. Carroll, "Luke's portrayal of the Pharisees," *Catholic Biblical Quarterly* 50 (1988): 604-621. Carroll points out that Jesus in Luke often criticizes Pharisees for their exclusivity. He says that the kingdom of God is open to all who repent, Pharisees and Gentiles alike.

15. It is generally agreed that John uses "the Jews" for a group of Jewish leaders who exercise authority among their people and are especially hostile to Jesus and his disciples.

16. John T. Townsend, "The Gospel of John and the Jews," in *Anti-Semitism and the Foundations of Christianity*, ed. by Alan Davies (New York: Paulist Press, 1979), 80-81; Smith, 83-88.

Chapter 4: Negative Accounts of Pharisees in the Gospels

1. Babylonian Talmud Berakhoth 28b, from Joachim Jeremias, *The Parables of Jesus,* trans. by S. H. Hooke (New York: Charles Scribner's Sons, 1955), 113.

2. Jeremias, 112; cf. Matt. 23:23.

3. Robert Ferrar Capon, "The Pharisee and the Publican," *The Reformed Journal*, Jan. 1988:11.

4. Capon, 11.

5. Matthew mentions them 10 times with Pharisees, and 12 times without them. Mark mentions them with Pharisees 3 times, and 18 times without them. Luke mentions them with Pharisees 5 times, and without them 9 times. John mentions them only once, and that is in conjunction with the Pharisees.

6. Anthony J. Saldarini, 241-276, esp. summary on 273-276.

7. Pheme Perkins, *Resurrection: New Testament Witness and Contemporary Reflection* (Garden City, N.Y.: Doubleday and Co., 1984), 204-205.

8. Saldarini, 223, 279. See also George Foot Moore, *Judaism in the First Centuries of the Christian Era*, vol. 2 (Cambridge: Harvard University Press, 1958), 193-194. Cf. Mishnah Sotah 3.5; Yadaim 4.6-8. Both the Babylonian and Jerusalem Talmuds list seven types of Pharisees, referring to all but one type with disapproval. Most of the criticisms have to do with hypocrisy and improper motives for studying the Torah. Hence, one should credit humility to the Talmudic writers, descended from the Pharisaic tradition as they were.

9. Mishnah Aboth 1.1.

10. Helmer Ringgren, *Religions of the Ancient Near East* (Philadelphia: Westminster Press, 1974), 164.

11. Patricia Klein, Evelyn Bence, et al. (Tappan, N.J.: Fleming H. Revell Company, 1987), 86.

12. Matt. 23:35 is the only other place mentioning lawyers in the Gospels.

13. Saldarini, 182-184.
14. Sherman E. Johnson, *The Gospel According to St. Matthew*, The Interpreter's Bible (Nashville: Abingdon Press, 1951), 7:530.
15. *Encyclopedia of World Methodism,* vol. 1 (Nashville: United Methodist Publishing House, 1974), 876-877.
16. See, however, note 18, on Matt. 23:15.
17. Matt. 23:14 does not appear in the best ancient Greek manuscripts, and many English translations leave it out. It was probably borrowed from Mark 12:40, where Jesus says that the scribes "devour widows' houses and for the sake of appearance say long prayers. They will receive the greater condemnation" (cf. Matt. 6:5).
18. E. P. Sanders mentions Matt. 23:15 in his criticism of scholars who have handed down the myth over the centuries that all Pharisees were rigidly exclusive and wanted no contact with "common" folk. He believes it is doubtful that there were many Pharisees traveling over land and sea to win converts (there weren't that many Pharisees to begin with). But Pharisee "evangelists" seem to have existed. *Judaism: Practice and Belief* (Philadelphia: Trinity Press International, 1992), 428-429.
19. Jacob Neusner, *From Politics to Piety,* pp. 38-39.
20. Günther Bornkamm, *Paul,* trans. by D. M. G. Stalker (New York: Harper & Row, 1971), 10. See also Lohse, 125.
21. Johnson, 34.
22. Johnson, 534-535. Mishnah Shebuoth 3.1—7.8 explains what oaths make one culpable and describes penalties for swearing falsely. See also the restrictions on oaths described in the Hebrew Bible: Exod. 20:7; Lev. 6:2-7; 19:12; Num. 30:3-15; Deut. 5:11; 23:22-23; Ps. 24:4; Jer. 5:2; 7:9; Mal. 3:5. The Essenes' attitude toward oath-taking seems to parallel Jesus'. Josephus mentions that the Essenes avoided swearing oaths: "They esteem it worse than perjury; for they say that he who cannot be believed without [swearing by] God is already condemned." *War of the Jews* 2.8.6, trans. by Whiston.
23. Neusner, *From Politics to Piety,* 79.
24. Johnson, 535. In commenting on the parallel passage in Luke, S. Maclean Gilmour notes that the Talmud specifically exempts rue from the tithe; *The Interpreter's Bible Commentary,* 8:216. See Mishnah Shebiith 9.1. On tithing, see esp. Mishnah Maaseroth and Mishnah Maaser Sheni.
25. Gerd Thiessen, *Sociology of Earliest Palestinian Christianity,* trans. by John Bowden (Philadelphia: Fortress Press, 1978), 43-44.
26. Neusner, *From Politics to Piety,* 85. Alexandrian wheat was also declared ritually unclean. The sixth division of the Mishnah, Tohoroth (Cleannesses), deals with what is clean and unclean and occupies about a fourth of the whole Mishnah.
27. Lohse, 78.
28. Lawrence Schiffman, in an address given at the Jewish Community Center, Rochester, N.Y., 10/31/92. In a follow-up letter dated 9/11/93, Schiffman referred to Mishnah Yadaim 4.7; cf. Mishnah Makshirin 5.9. He also cited J. M. Baumgarten's article in *Journal of Jewish Studies* 31 (1980): 163-164.
29. Johnson, 537. See also Mishnah Maaser Sheni 5.1; Shekalim 1.1; Moed Katan 1.2; Oholoth has much on contracting uncleanness from corpses, building on Num. 19, esp. 19:14.
30. Johnson, 264.

Chapter 5: How Jesus' Critique of the Pharisees Applies to Us

1. *Oxford English Dictionary*, vol. XI (Oxford: Clarendon Press, 1989), 661-662; used by permission.

2. (New York: Seaview Books, 1980), 56.

3. Doris Janzen Longacre, *Living More with Less*, Scottdale, Pa.: Herald Press, 1980.

4. See Mishnah Shabbat.

5. On dancing in celebration, see 1 Sam. 30:16; Ps. 30:11; Luke 15:25. Dancing could be part of celebrating the true worship of the Lord (Exod. 15:20; 2 Sam. 6:14; Ps. 150:4) or false worship (Exod. 32:19). Some may argue that the dancing in these verses does not necessarily relate to contemporary social dancing of men and women together. However, the Bible nowhere forbids dancing of any sort.

6. *Consumer Reports*, July 1992:414.

7. "United States: Capital Punishment," *Facts on File*, 12/3/92, vol. 52:913. "Death Row Medication Curbed," *Facts on File*, 11/23/90, vol. 50:869. A person at the Washington Office of the National Coalition to Abolish the Death Penalty also recommended the articles "Fit to Kill?" in *The New York Times*, Nov. 15, 1990; and "Justices Order State to Review Medicating Death Row Insane," in *The Washington Post*, Nov. 13, 1990.

Chapter 6: Christendom's Persecution of the Jews

1. Irwin Borowsky, "Preface to Second Edition," in Simon Wiesenthal's *Every Day Remembrance Day: a Chronicle of Jewish Martyrdom* (New York: Henry Holt and Company, 1986; Philadelphia: American Interfaith Institute, 1992).

2. Gerd Thiessen, *Sociology of Early Palestinian Christianity*, trans. by John Bowden (Philadelphia: Fortress Press, 1978), 92-93; Victor Tcherikover, *Hellenistic Civilization and the Jews*, trans. by S. Applebaum (Philadelphia: Jewish Publication Society of America, 1959), 357-377 on Hellenistic anti-Semitism.

3. See John 9:22; 12:42; 16:2.

4. Edward H. Flannery, *The Anguish of the Jews: Twenty-Three Centuries of Anti-Semitism* (New York: Paulist Press, 1985), 36. It should be noted that there are few documented accounts of Jewish violence against Christians in the first three centuries. Christians suffered many more casualties at the hands of pagans in the Roman empire.

5. Flannery, 37.

6. Malcolm Hay, *Europe and the Jews: The Pressure of Christendom on the People of Israel for 1900 Years* (Boston: Beacon Press, 1960), 25-26. Hay's book appeared originally in 1950 under the title of *Foot of Pride* (from Ps. 36:11).

7. Hay, 27-31.

8. Henry Chadwick, *The Early Church* (Harmondsworth, England: Penguin Books, 1967), 125-127.

9. Hay, 37.

10. Hay, 41-43.

11. Hay, 122-123.

12. Hay, 75-76.

13. Hay, 81.

14. Hay, 87.

15. Barbara W. Tuchman, *A Distant Mirror: The Calamitous 14th Century* (New York: Ballantine Books, 1978), 112.

16. Hay, 120.

17. Hay, 112.
18. Hay, 145.
19. Hay, 117-119.
20. Hay, 99.
21. Hay, 94-95. Cf. *The Merchant of Venice*, by William Shakespeare.
22. Hay, 99.
23. Hay, 107.
24. Hay, 109.
25. Hay, 121.
26. Hay, 73.
27. Hay, 127.
28. Hay, 142.
29. Hay, 142-143.
30. Tuchman, 109.
31. Tuchman, 483-484.
32. Hay, 157.
33. Tuchman, 113-114.
34. Israel Abrahams, *Jewish Life in the Middle Ages* (Philadelphia: Jewish Publication Society, 1958), 418.
35. Hay, 148-149.
36. Hay, 151.
37. Hay, 153.
38. Frank Ephraim Talmage, ed., *Disputation and Dialogue: Readings in the Jewish Christian Encounter* (New York: KTAV Publishing House, 1975), 34-35.
39. Hay, 165.
40. Hay, 165-166.
41. Wiesenthal, 137.
42. Hay, 170-171.
43. Hay, 166.
44. Hay, 131.
45. Hay, 131.
46. Hay, 131.
47. Wiesenthal, 53.
48. Hay, 311.
49. Hay, 176-182.
50. Hay, 134.
51. Hay, 194-195.
52. Hay, 199.
53. Hay, 196.
54. *The New Encyclopaedia Britannica*, 15th ed., *Micropaedia* (Chicago: Encyclopaedia Britannica, 1991), IX:742.
55. Hay, 201-204.
56. Hay, 160.
57. Hay, 52-53.
58. Hay, 139.
59. John S. Conway, *The Nazi Persecution of the Churches* (New York: Basic Books, 1968), 26.
60. Conway, 410-411.
61. Conway, 226-227.
62. Taylor first paraphrased Paul's letters in 1962, the prophetic books in 1965, the Gospels in 1966, and so on. Interestingly, when Tyndale House Pub-

lishers (Wheaton, Illinois) brought out the complete *Living Bible: Paraphrased* in 1971, Taylor's name appeared nowhere on or in the book.

63. Eldon J. Epp "Jews and Judaism in *The Living New Testament*," in *Biblical and Near Eastern Studies: Essays in Honor of William Sanford LaSor*, ed. by Gary A. Tuttle (Grand Rapids: William B. Eerdmans Publishing Company, 1978), 86.

64. *The Great Hatred* (New York: Alfred A. Knopf, 1940), 127-128.

65. Rosemary Radford Ruether writes, "Christians can hope that prophets will rise in Israel to [address the victimization of the Palestinians] to their people in power. But they cannot well imagine that they themselves are the prophets. As the crucifixes drenched with Jewish blood drop from our hands, we stand impotent and wordless before this tragedy of Israel and Palestine. . . . In the name of the crucified Messiah, we must struggle against the conditions which make history a trail of crucifixions. Only then, in solidarity with Jews and Palestinians, can we dream of Messianic times, of a shalom without victims." From her essay in *Anti-Semitism and the Foundations of Christianity*, ed. by Alan Davies (New York: Paulist Press, 1979), 255-256.

66. Emil L. Fackenheim, "The People Israel Lives," in *Disputation and Dialogue*, ed. by Talmage, 307.

67. Robert P. Eriksen, *Theologians Under Hitler* (New Haven: Yale University Press, 1985), 42.

Chapter 7: Toward Humility and Dialogue

1. The book of Job was written to answer the question, "Why does God allow bad things to happen to those who love him and follow his commandments?"

2. "Judaism in the Post-Christian Era," in *Disputation and Dialogue*, ed. by Talmage, 293.

3. Rosemary Ruether, *Faith and Fratricide: The Theological Roots of Anti-Semitism* (New York: Seabury Press, 1974), 259-260.

4. "The New Testament and Judaism: An Historical Perspective on the Theme," *Review and Expositor* 84 (Spring 1987): 184-185.

5. "No Religion Is an Island," *Disputation and Dialogue*, ed. by Talmage, 350.

6. By Thieleman J. van Braght (Scottdale, Pa.: Herald Press, 1938; original Dutch edition, 1600).

7. Scottdale, Pa.: Herald Press, 1979.

8. Kuiper was instrumental in starting a Christian kibbutz in Galilee. In 1987 many Dutch Mennonites objected to placing "collective guilt" upon Jews for the death of Jesus (using Matt. 27:25) and confessed their own guilt of silence in the 1930s for not protesting the Nazi death camps. See Jacob J. Enz, "Judaism and Jews," in *The Mennonite Encyclopedia*, vol. 5, ed. by C. J. Dyck et al. (Scottdale, Pa.: Herald Press, 1990), 469-470.

9. Reported from personal conversation between Zev Garber and S. David Garber at the meetings of the American Academy of Religon and the Society of Biblical Literature at New Orleans in November 1990. Zev Garber teaches in the department of Jewish studies of the Los Angeles Valley College.

10. Israel Abrahams, *Jewish Life in the Middle Ages* (Philadelphia: Jewish Publication Society, 1958), 408.

11. Cornelius J. Dyck, *An Introduction to Mennonite History* (Scottdale, Pa.: Herald Press, 1981), 186. German domination of the Ukraine became progressively more despotic as World War II continued—for the Mennonite settlements as well as the other inhabitants of the region.

12. Perry Yoder, professor of Old Testament at Associated Mennonite Biblical Seminaries, believes that Anabaptist biblical scholars can benefit from learning Jewish methods of Scripture interpretation. Traditional mainstream Christian scholarship, while developing critical methods for academic understanding of the Hebrew Bible, has often failed to develop satisfactory methods of helping lay people interpret it to affect their values, theology, and behavior. Since the Anabaptists modeled themselves on a largely Jewish early Christian church, it behooves them to employ the practical methods of interpreting Hebrew Scripture used by the early church and those used by many Jewish scholars today. "The Importance of Judaism for Contemporary Anabaptist Thought," *Mennonite Quarterly Review* 67 (January 1993): 73-83.

13. "The New Testament and Judaism: An Historical Perspective on a Theme," *Review and Expositor* 84 (Spring 1987): 197.

14. David L. Schiedermayer, "Choices in Plague Time," *Christianity Today*, Aug. 7, 1987:22.

Bibliography

ABD: *Anchor Bible Dictionary, The*. Ed. by D. N. Freedman et al. 6 vols. New York: Doubleday, 1992.

Abrahams, Israel. *Jewish Life in the Middle Ages*. Philadelphia: Jewish Publication Society, 1958.

Atlas of Jerusalem. New York: Walter Degruyter, 1973.

Aune, D. E. "On the Origins of the 'Council of Javneh' Myth." *Journal of Biblical Literature* 110 (Fall 1991): 491-493.

Barrett, C. K. *The New Testament Background: Selected Documents*. New York: Harper & Row, 1961.

Baumgarten, A. I. "The Name of the Pharisees." *Journal of Biblical Literature* 102 (1983): 411-428.

______________. "The Pharisaic *Paradosis*." *Harvard Theological Review* 80 (no. 1, 1987): 63-77.

Baumgarten, Joseph M. "The Pharisaic Controversies About Purity and the Qumran Texts." *Journal of Jewish Studies* (Autumn 1980): 157-170.

Bergmann, Martin S. *In the Shadow of Moloch: The Sacrifice of Children and Its Impact on Western Religions.* New York: Columbia University Press, 1992.

Berkovits, Eliezer. "Judaism in the Post-Christian Era." In *Disputation and Dialogue*. *See* Talmage.

Bettenson, Henry, ed. *Documents of the Christian Church.* 2nd ed. London: Oxford University Press, 1963.

Bornkamm, Günther. *Paul.* Trans. by D. M. G. Stalker. New York: Harper & Row, 1971.

Boulton, Wayne G. *Is Legalism a Heresy?* New York: Paulist Press, 1982.

Bowker, John. *Jesus and the Pharisees*. Cambridge: University Press, 1973.

Bright, John. *A History of Israel*. 3d ed. Philadelphia: Westminster Press, 1981.

Brittain, Vera. *Testament of Youth.* New York: Seaview Books, 1980.

Burrows, Millar. *The Dead Sea Scrolls*. New York: Viking Press, 1961.
Capon, Robert Ferrar. "The Pharisee and the Publican." *Reformed Journal* 38 (Jan. 1988): 11-14.
Carroll, John T. "Luke's Portrayal of the Pharisees." *Catholic Biblical Quarterly* 50 (1988): 604-621.
Chadwick, Henry. *The Early Church*. Harmondsworth, England: Penguin Books, 1967.
Charlesworth, James H. "Is the New Testament Anti-Semitic or Anti-Jewish?" *Explorations* 7 (no. 2, 1993): 2-3.
Cochrane, Arthur C. *The Church's Confession Under Hitler*. Pittsburgh: The Pickwick Press, 1976.
Coleman, William L. *Those Pharisees*. New York: Hawthorn Books, 1977.
Conway, John S. *The Nazi Persecution of the Churches*. New York: Basic Books, 1968.
Cook, Donald. "A Gospel Portrait of the Pharisees." *Review and Expositor* 84:221-233.
Cook, Michael. "The New Testament and Judaism: A Historical Perspective on the Theme." *Review and Expositor* 84 (Spring 1987):183-199.
Culpepper, Alan. "The Gospel of John and the Jews." *Review and Expositor* 84 (Spring 1987): 273-288.
Davies, Alan, ed. *Anti-Semitism and the Foundations of Christianity*. New York: Paulist Press, 1979.
Davies, W. D. *The Gospel and the Land: Early Christianity and Jewish Territorial Doctrine*. Berkeley: University of California Press, 1974.
________________. *The Setting of the Sermon on the Mount*. Brown Judaic Studies, 186. Atlanta: Scholars Press, 1989.
Dead Sea Scrolls in English, The. Trans. by G. Vermes. 3d ed. New York: Penguin Books, 1987.
Dyck, Cornelius J. *An Introduction to Mennonite History*. Scottdale: Herald Press, 1981
Encyclopedia Judaica. Jerusalem: Keter Publishing House, 1971.
Encyclopedia of World Methodism. Nashville: United Methodist Publishing House, 1974.
Enz, Jacob J. "Judaism and Jews," *The Mennonite Encyclopedia* 5:469-470. *See* ME.
Epp, Eldon J. "Jews and Judaism in *The Living New Testament*." In *Biblical and Near Eastern Studies: Essays in Honor of William Sanford LaSor*. Ed. by Gary A. Tuttle. Grand Rapids, Mich.: William B. Eerdmans Publishing Company, 1978.
Eriksen, Robert P. *Theologians Under Hitler*. New Haven: Yale University Press, 1985.
Fackenheim, Emil L. "The People Israel Lives." In *Disputation and Dialogue*. *See* Talmage.
Falk, Harvey. *Jesus the Pharisee: A New Look at the Jewishness of Jesus*. New York: Paulist Press, 1985.
Finkelstein, Louis. *The Pharisees*. 2 vols. Philadelphia: The Jewish Publication Society of America, 1938, 1962.
Flannery, Edward H. *The Anguish of the Jews: Twenty-Three Centuries of Anti-Semitism*. New York: Paulist Press, 1985.
Hay, Malcolm. *Europe and the Jews: The Pressure of Christendom on the People of Israel for 1900 Years*. Boston: Beacon Press, 1960.

Herford, R. Travers. *The Truth About the Pharisees.* Menorah Pamphlets, 3. New York: Intercollegiate Menorah Association, 1925.

Heschel, Abraham. "No Man Is an Island." In *Disputation and Dialogue. See* Talmage.

Howard, Wilbert F. *The Gospel According to St. John.* The Interpreter's Bible, 8. Nashville: Abingdon Press, 1952.

Isaac, Jules. *The Teaching of Contempt: Christian Roots of Anti-Semitism.* New York: Holt, Rinehart and Winston, 1964.

Jeremias, Joachim. *The Parables of Jesus.* Trans. by S. H. Hooke. New York: Charles Scribner's Sons, 1955.

Johnson, Sherman E. *The Gospel According to St. Matthew.* The Interpreter's Bible, 7. Nashville: Abingdon Press, 1951.

Josephus. *The Life and Works of Flavius Josephus*. Trans. by William Whiston. Peabody, Mass.: Hendrickson, 1987 (or from other publishers).

Jospe, Raphael, and Stanley M. Wagner, eds. *Great Schisms in Jewish History.* New York: KTAV Publishing House, 1981.

Katz, Jacob. *From Prejudice to Destruction: Anti-Semitism, 1700-1933*. Cambridge: Harvard University Press, 1980.

Lohse, Eduard. *The New Testament Environment*. Nashville: Abingdon, 1976.

ME: *The Mennonite Encyclopedia*. Vols. 1-4, ed. by H. S. Bender et al., 1955-59; vol. 5, ed. by C. J. Dyck et al., 1990; Scottdale, Pa.: Herald Press.

Moore, George Foote. *Judaism in the First Centuries of the Christian Era.* 3 vols. Cambridge, Mass.: Harvard Univ. Press, 1927-30.

The Mishnah. Trans. by Herbert Danby. London: Oxford U. Press, 1933.

Neusner, Jacob. *From Politics to Piety: The Emergence of Pharisaic Judaism*. Englewood Cliffs, N.J.: Prentice Hall, 1973.

Oakman, Douglas E. *Jesus and the Economic Questions of His Day.* Lewiston, N.Y.: Edwin Mellen Press, 1986.

Oxford English Dictionary. 2d ed. Oxford: Clarendon Press, 1989.

Oyer, John S., and Robert S. Kreider. *The Mirror of the Martyrs.* Intercourse, Pa.: Good Books, 1990.

Perkins, Pheme. *Resurrection: New Testament Witness and Contemporary Reflection.* Garden City, N.Y.: Doubleday, 1984.

Perrin, Norman. *Rediscovering the Teachings of Jesus.* New York: Harper & Row, 1967.

Perrin, Norman, and Dennis C. Duling. *The New Testament: An Introduction*. 2nd ed. New York: Harcourt Brace Jovanovich, 1982.

Ringgren, Helmer. *Religions of the Ancient Near East.* Philadelphia: Westminster Press, 1974.

Robinson, John A. T. *Redating the New Testament.* Philadelphia: Westminster Press, 1976.

Roetzel, Calvin J. *The Letters of Paul: Conversations in Context.* Atlanta: John Knox Press, 1982.

Rosenbaum, Ron. "Riddle of the Scrolls." *Vanity Fair*, Nov. 1992: 222-228, 286-294.

Ruether, Rosemary. *Faith and Fratricide: The Theological Roots of Anti-Semitism.* New York: Seabury Press, 1974.

_______________. "The Faith and Fratricide Discussion: Old Problems and New Dimensions." In *Anti-Semitism and. . . . See* Davies, Alan, 230-256.

Saldarini, Anthony J. *Pharisees, Scribes and Sadducees.* Wilmington: Michael Glazier, 1988.

Samuel, Maurice. *The Great Hatred.* New York: Alfred A. Knopf, 1940.
Sanders, E. P. *Judaism: Practice and Belief.* Philadelphia: Trinity Press International, 1992.
Schiffman, Lawrence H. "Jewish Sectarianism in Second Temple Times." In *Great Schisms in Jewish History.* Ed. by Raphael Jospe and Stanley M. Wagner. Denver: Center for Judaic Studies, 1981:1-46.
________________. "New Light on the Pharisees: Insights from the Dead Sea Scrolls," *Bible Review* 8 (June 1992): 30-33, 54.
________________. "The Significance of the Scrolls." *Bible Review* 6 (Oct. 1990): 19-27.
________________. *Who Was a Jew? Rabbinic and Halakhic Perspectives on the Jewish-Christian Schism.* Hoboken, N.J.: KTAV Publishing House, 1985.
Schniedermayer, David L. "Choices in Plague Time." *Christianity Today,* Aug. 7, 1987:22.
Schwartz, Daniel R. *Studies in the Jewish Background of Christianity.* Tübingen, Germany: J. C. B. Mohr, 1992.
Segal, Alan F. *Paul the Convert: The Apostolate and Apostasy of Saul the Pharisee.* Yale University Press, 1990.
Smith, D. Moody. "Judaism and the Gospel of John." In *Jews and Christians: Exploring the Past, Present, and Future.* Ed. by James H. Charlesworth et al. New York: Crossroad, 1990:76-96.
Smucker, Barbara Claassen. *Days of Terror.* Harmondsworth, England: Puffin Books, 1981.
Snoek, Johan M. *The Grey Book: A Collection of Protests Against Anti-Semitism and the Persecution of the Jews Issued by the Non-Roman Catholic Churches and Church Leaders During Hitler's Rule.* New York: Humanities Press, 1970.
Talmadge, Frank Ephraim, ed. *Disputation and Dialogue: Readings in the Jewish-Christian Encounter.* New York: KTAV Publishing House, 1975.
Tcherikover, Victor. *Hellenistic Civilization and the Jews.* Trans. by S. Applebaum. Philadelphia: Jewish Publication Society of America, 1959.
Thiessen, Gerd. *Sociology of Earliest Palestinian Christianity.* Trans. by John Bowden. Philadelphia: Fortress Press, 1978.
Thompson, J. A. *The Bible and Archaeology.* 3d ed. Grand Rapids, Mich.: William B. Eerdmans, 1982.
Townsend, John T. "The Gospel of John and the Jews: The Story of a Religious Divorce." In *Anti-Semitism and. . . . See* Davies, Alan, 72-97.
Tuchman, Barbara W. *A Distant Mirror: The Calamitous Fourteenth Century.* New York: Ballantine Books, 1978.
Viviano, Benedict T., and Justin Taylor. "Sadducees, Angels, and the Resurrection." *Journal of Biblical Literature* 111 (Fall 1992): 496-498.
Webster's New Collegiate Dictionary. Springfield, Mass.: G. and C. Merriam Company, 1977.
Wiesenthal, Simon. *Every Day Remembrance Day: A Chronicle of Jewish Martyrdom.* New York: Henry Holt and Company, 1986; Philadelphia: American Interfaith Institute, 1992.
Yoder, Perry. "The Importance of Judaism for Contemporary Anabaptist Thought." *Mennonite Quarterly Review* 67 (Jan. 1993): 73-83.
Zahn, Gordon C. *The German Catholics and Hitler's Wars.* New York: E. P. Dutton, 1969.

The Author

Kathleen Kern has written Bible curriculum material for the Mennonite Publishing House and cooperative publishers, released in the *Adult Bible Study Guide,* the *Builder,* and the Foundation Series for youth. She has also written for *Workman Quarterly.*

Kern received a B.A. from Bluffton (Ohio) College and an M.A. in biblical studies from Colgate Rochester (N.Y.) Divinity School. Her first book, *Getting to Know the Old Testament,* appeared in 1990 as part of the Foundation Series for youth. *When It Hurts to Live,* forty biblical devotions for Christians struggling with depression, was published by Faith & Life Press in 1994. Her fiction has appeared in *The Door,* and she has had articles and poetry published in the *Gospel Herald, The Other Side,* and various other denominational publications. Through her writing, Kern seeks to empower people of all ages to take the Bible seriously and see its intense relevance for their lives and for society.

For five years Kern worked with developmentally disabled adults. In 1993 she began serving as a member of the Christian Peacemaker Corps. This group is dedicated to intervening in violent situations using biblical principles of nonviolent direction action. When not on roving assignment in places such as Haiti, Chicago, or Washington (D.C.), she lives in the Rochester, New York, area and pursues her writing career. Kern is a member of the Rochester Area Mennonite Fellowship.